"Over the years, one of the things I've enjoyed most about being a public speaker is having opportunities to hang out with Carey. We've had dozens of meals and more coffees than I can count. I've had the good fortune to hear these ideas as they developed and as they've helped leaders across the country. It's not a matter of if you'll run into these challenges; it's a matter of when. Be prepared by spending a little time with a leader who has already been there."

—JON ACUFF, *New York Times* best-selling author
    of *Finish: Give Yourself the Gift of Done*

"Burnout, cynicism, disconnection, compromise—are these just the inevitable curses of growing older in a rapidly changing, technology-addicted world? Carey Nieuwhof believes we can see these ills coming before they befall us and can take steps to avoid them. If you're looking for gentle, empathetic life coaching from a Christian perspective, this book is sure to help you."

—DANIEL H. PINK, *New York Times* best-selling author
    of *When* and *Drive*

"One of the biggest challenges of the Christian life is staying the course. Experiences happening to us and around us every day try to derail us. In this book, Carey will help you identify some of the biggest distractions threatening to keep you from your God-given destiny and will provide you with tools to redirect your focus and keep your eyes fixed on Jesus so you can finish your race strong."

—CHRISTINE CAINE, best-selling author and founder
    of A21 and Propel Women

"Leaders do well when they continually examine themselves, and they set themselves up for failure when they don't. Carey points leaders to some very important areas to observe."

—DR. HENRY CLOUD, leadership consultant and author
    of *The Power of the Other*

"If you don't take the time to see what's coming at you, you can't see the One who's coming for you. And that's why you have to read this book, which hands you more than binoculars. Carey Nieuwhof offers you his own beckoning hand. And he is an uncommonly perceptive and generous guide whose fresh, luminous insights are a needed lens for all leaders to scout out more courage, more capacity, more Christ."

— ANN VOSKAMP, *New York Times* best-selling author
of *The Broken Way* and *One Thousand Gifts*

"Carey isn't just a great lawyer; he's a wise friend. This is a practical book about navigating your life. With clarity and authenticity, Carey reminds us it usually isn't the destination that's the problem. It's the distractions along the way that will get us off course."

— BOB GOFF, *New York Times* best-selling author
of *Love Does* and *Everybody, Always*

"Life has a way of broadsiding us with lessons that we need to learn but would rather avoid. In his new book, *Didn't See It Coming*, Carey Nieuwhof candidly addresses seven key life challenges that every leader will face. Carey writes with deep biblical insight, straightforward truth, and practical wisdom to help you grow despite facing life's obstacles."

— CRAIG GROESCHEL, pastor and *New York Times*
best-selling author

"Carey is a deep thinker with a significant contemporary voice developed from his unique life journey. Through seasons of idealism and cynicism, disillusionment and burnout, Carey has navigated a path through unexpected and enormous challenges to become an influential leader and minister of the gospel. He leads from his life and relationship with Jesus Christ with engaging humility and disarming vulnerability. Carey has carefully and generously assembled the wisdom he has garnered along the way into this powerful, personal, and highly readable book."

— BRIAN HOUSTON, global senior pastor of Hillsong Church
and author of *There Is More*

"Whether you're in the corner office or just getting started as a leader, this book will become one of your greatest allies in your march toward success. In *Didn't See It Coming*, Carey Nieuwhof tackles seven life issues that blindside way too many leaders. Whatever challenge you're facing, whatever obstacle you're hoping to overcome, whatever future you dream or imagine, there is something powerful for you here."

—ANDY STANLEY, author, communicator, and founder
of North Point Ministries

"At some point every leader struggles with deeper issues—soul issues, heart issues, life issues. I've known Carey Nieuwhof for a long time and have seen him navigate these matters with humility, skill, and effectiveness. *Didn't See It Coming* is a masterful treatment of some of the biggest challenges you'll ever face, and Carey offers you the wisdom and strategies to tackle them."

—REGGIE JOINER, CEO of Orange

"Carey Nieuwhof is one of my favorite people on the planet for a few reasons. First, he's the genuine article. Second, he challenges the way I think. I believe you'll feel the same way after reading this book! Few people see the future as clearly as Carey. He will help you not only see a better future but also create it."

—MARK BATTERSON, *New York Times* best-selling
author of *The Circle Maker* and lead pastor of
National Community Church

"Buckle up, friends! What Carey Nieuwhof has shared in these pages is everything you secretly fear and exactly what you need to hear. Too many of us (myself included) have come dangerously close to being crippled by these seven challenges. Your leadership influence is a sacred responsibility and requires a deep commitment to lead yourself well. If you're brave enough to do the hard work, this book will be the lifeline you need to keep leading well for the long haul!"

—JENNI CATRON, founder of the 4Sight Group

"Communication skills are only half the battle in leadership and life. If we're honest, the real struggle happens inside our hearts and souls. Nieuwhof's new book provides expert guidance in the life issues that make or break us as leaders and as people. He addresses each issue honestly and with an accuracy that pierces the heart."

> —NANCY DUARTE, best-selling author and CEO
> of Duarte Inc.

"Carey Nieuwhof cares deeply about leaders and proves it with this challenging yet hopeful book. We all need a guide to help us know what's around the corner in our leadership journey, and Carey provides helpful perspective for any leader at any level."

> —BRAD LOMENICK, author of *H3 Leadership* and
> *The Catalyst Leader* and former president of Catalyst

"It's been said that youth is wasted on the young and wisdom wasted on the old. But what if the wisdom of age and experience could be transferred to anyone still on the journey? That's exactly what Carey Nieuwhof has done in *Didn't See It Coming*. If you're interested in accelerating your growth as a leader and learning wisdom beyond your years, pick up a copy today."

> —WILLIAM VANDERBLOEMEN, founder and CEO
> of Vanderbloemen Search Group

"Carey is one of my favorite church leadership voices. If you want to know what the future holds and how to react to it tomorrow, read *Didn't See It Coming* today."

> —JOHN ORTBERG, senior pastor of Menlo Church and
> author of *I'd Like You More If You Were More Like Me*

DIDN'T SEE IT COMING

OVERCOMING THE 7 GREATEST CHALLENGES
THAT NO ONE EXPECTS
AND EVERYONE EXPERIENCES

CAREY NIEUWHOF

WATERBROOK

DIDN'T SEE IT COMING

This book is not intended to replace the advice of a trained psychological or medical professional. Readers are advised to consult a qualified professional regarding treatment. The author and publisher specifically disclaim liability, loss, or risk, personal or otherwise, which is incurred as a consequence, directly or indirectly, of the use or application of any of the contents of this book.

All Scripture quotations are taken from the Holy Bible, New Living Translation, copyright © 1996, 2004, 2007, 2013, 2015 by Tyndale House Foundation. Used by permission of Tyndale House Publishers Inc., Carol Stream, Illinois 60188. All rights reserved.

Details in some anecdotes and stories have been changed to protect the identities of the persons involved.

Library of Congress Cataloging-in-Publication Data
Names: Nieuwhof, Carey, author.
Title: Didn't see it coming : overcoming the seven greatest challenges that no one expects and everyone experiences / Carey Nieuwhof.
Description: First edition. | Colorado Springs : WaterBrook, 2018. | Includes bibliographical references.
Identifiers: LCCN 2018000541 | ISBN 9780735291331 (hardcover) | ISBN 9780735291348 (ebook)
Subjects: LCSH: Expectation (Psychology)—Religious aspects—Christianity. | Surprise. | Christian life.
Classification: LCC BV4647.E93 N54 2018 | DDC 248.8/6—dc23
LC record available at https://lccn.loc.gov/2018000541

Printed in the United States of America
2018—First Edition

10 9 8 7 6 5 4 3 2 1

SPECIAL SALES
Most WaterBrook books are available at special quantity discounts when purchased in bulk by corporations, organizations, and special-interest groups. Custom imprinting or excerpting can also be done to fit special needs. For information, please e-mail specialmarketscms@penguinrandomhouse.com or call 1-800-603-7051.

To my wife, Toni

I knew there was something amazing in you from the first time I laid eyes on you. I just had no idea it could be this deep, this rich, or this profound for this long. Not to mention this much fun. And to think we're just getting started.

And to my parents, Marten and Marja

Your constant encouragement, support, faith, and love never cease to encourage me and inspire me. You always point the way toward hope and toward Jesus.

Contents

Introduction

SURPRISE

No one in his or her twenties sets out to end up feeling empty or cynical. At least I didn't. I don't know of any college graduates who want to become irrelevant and morally compromised before their fortieth birthday. I can't imagine men and women at any age who want their personal relationships to collapse under the weight of pride or the lack of basic emotional intelligence.

Yet each of those things happens every day to people we know. People we care about. People we love. Actually, it might be happening to you right now, though you remain completely unaware. Because that's exactly how it happens.

The implosions often come as a surprise. That's what happened to me. And I've seen the unexpected issues we deal with in this book flatten many good people.

They simply didn't see it coming.

They didn't see the edge of burnout before they hit it.

They didn't see their marriage becoming distant and desperately disconnected.

They didn't see the compromise they made at work coming until they knew they had crossed a line of no return.

They didn't see that their once cutting-edge style and insight had become insufferably stale.

They didn't imagine the emptiness they would feel after all their dreams came true.

They just didn't see it coming. Few of us do.

The question I want to tackle in this book is, Could they have seen it coming? Can you?

SHOW ME A SIGN

Let's ask a difficult and personal set of questions: Are there signs? Do you have to be blindsided again and again? Are there clues along the way you can detect to save yourself from heartache, loss, and pain?

If you're heading into a challenging season, is there any way to know you're moving in that direction before it's too late? Are there signs you can watch for that will help you avoid the problems so many well-meaning people stumble into? Could you know if you're the top candidate for Most Cynical Person on the Planet? Are there clues that you're going to become the forty-five-year-old leader no one listens to anymore? Are there signs that you're en route to becoming incredibly successful and desperately empty at the same time?

The way most people get into these unintended places is simple: They miss the warning signs. They don't see it coming. The good news is that you *can* see it coming. This book is for people who want to see the signs that there's a major life challenge ahead before it's too late.

When I first started sharing at conferences some of the ideas that became this book, I thought I was addressing people forty and over. The first time I gave a talk on cynicism in front of a thousand leaders in Atlanta, I told the audience that anyone in their twenties and thirties would just need to squirrel this away for another day. Needless to say, I was shocked (and saddened) when, after my talk, a very long line of twentysomethings, many with tears in their eyes, said this was already their story. It broke my heart and made me realize that so many of the things that have now made their way into this book have become the epidemics of our age.

So I began to rethink the essence of my message. I now believe the signs we explore in this book exist for all of us, whatever stage of the journey we might be on. These warning signs, if recognized and heeded, are gifts from God to spare us from the self-inflicted sadness and heartbreak that mark too many lives these days.

Some chapters might sound like they're narrating your life. Scary as that might be, I pray they feel like hope to you. I want to be like a friend who comes into your living room and shines a light into the darkness, who points you in a direction that leads to fulfillment and meaning, who helps you anticipate storms ahead and provides strategies to weather them. Even if the crisis is not in full swing yet, the steps outlined here will save you significant heartache and trouble.

WHAT IF YOU'RE NOT THE RELIGIOUS TYPE?

It won't take you long to figure out this book was written from a Christian perspective. There's a good reason for that: I am a pastor, and more important, I try my best to live according to Jesus's teachings. Through many ups and downs in my own life, I have become convinced that he provides the fullest answer to our deepest longings and that he's the hope for this world. You might agree or disagree, but hear me out. There is more help here than you think, regardless of where you stand on matters of spirituality.

Before I became a pastor, I worked as a lawyer (more on that to come), so it's not exactly like I've lived in a religious bubble my whole life. If you don't consider yourself a religious person, I'm glad you're reading this. If you consider yourself *spiritual* but not specifically Christian, I'm glad you're reading this. What I saw in my brief time in law gave me a permanent affection for people who aren't that into church or Christianity, even for those who consider themselves atheists.

In fact, as a pastor I've spent more than two decades trying to build a church that people who don't go to church love to attend. I've been privileged over the years to see thousands of people who never thought they would end up in church end up in church. And to their utter surprise, many of them liked it. Many of them even discovered a relationship with Jesus.

I hope this book is an extension of that spirit. Maybe a friend gave you the book as a gift, or you heard a friend talk about it and you grabbed a copy. All I can say is welcome. I'm so glad you're here.

I believe you'll find that we all struggle with the same issues because, well, we're human. Christians can grow cynical. So can people who don't consider themselves Christians.

I've tried to strike a tone in this book that works for those who are skeptical of Christianity and for those who passionately follow Jesus. As a result, this book may end up not feeling Christian enough for those who are Christians and too Christian for those who aren't. If that's the case, I may have hit the mark.

I hope what you discover is a resource that is thoroughly biblical in its teachings without being preachy, thoroughly Christian in its framework while still being immensely practical and true to life. That's what authentic Christianity is anyway. So you'll encounter some chapters that have a bit of Bible. Others will have less. Either way, I hope what you read will help you dive into the meaning of life at its most profound level. Rather than pushing you away from a dialogue with God, I hope it moves you into one.

SOME HOPE

However you end up navigating this book, I pray it leaves you in the place where you realize you have a God and some friends who haven't given up on you. I hope you will be assured that you have people who believe in you, even if you've given up on them. Because that's what often happens when you find yourself in the places described in this book. You stop believing. And you need to recognize that there are people who know the kind of person you really are yet still decide to stay. Yep, they know you, and they love you anyway.

If any of that happens, just know it points to a bigger reality: there is a God who believes in you and sent his Son not just to die but also to live so that you might experience real life. That's what I hope this book does: points you toward the life that escapes so many. The Scriptures narrate a way of wisdom, a path God has set for us, that I have missed as often as I have hit. But if you take good notes and pay attention, both to how God works and to how life works, you can find a better path.

Cynicism, compromise, disconnection, irrelevance, pride, burnout, emptiness—none of these need to be your final story. You can see them coming. You can identify them when they arrive. And when you name them, when you see them, they lose some of their allure as well as their power.

If you do see the seven greatest challenges coming, you may end up living the life you've always hoped to live, which is the life that eludes too many.

PART I

CYNICISM

FIND ME A HAPPY LAWYER

How Cynicism Snuffs Out Hope

Y ou never thought you'd be a cynic, did you? It's not like in your sopho-
more year of high school beside your yearbook photo you wrote, "I
hope to grow jaded and distrustful of humanity by the time I hit forty. I'm
also hoping my cynicism will damage my family and make me impossible
to work with. *Go Ravens!*"

Had you written that in high school, somebody would have insisted
you go to counseling . . . immediately. But that wasn't your headspace. You
were optimistic, even hopeful. And by the time you hit your early twenties
and shed the yoke of your parents, you were downright *idealistic.* You knew
how to make the world a better place, and you were intent on doing it.

That's my story too. As a young law student working in downtown
Toronto, I oozed optimism about setting the world right. I wanted to
practice constitutional law and argue my first case before the Supreme
Court of Canada prior to my thirtieth birthday. I even discovered that
someone with a positive attitude and a healthy work ethic could make a
difference in a downtown firm. I was a newlywed, and halfway through

my first year at the law firm, I became a new dad. I wanted to be successful yet *not* work the slavishly long hours young lawyers were famous for, working every night and most weekends. Some firms in the downtown core even had cots in the office and hired in-house chefs so their employees didn't have to go home or leave the office. I didn't want that to be me.

So I hustled hard. I arrived at the office at seven o'clock, worked through lunch, and by five o'clock managed to sneak out of the office when no one was looking so I could get home to my wife, Toni, and our newborn son. Throughout the day, I focused on being massively productive and getting outcomes our clients (and my bosses) would love.

Strangely enough, I managed to succeed. My idealism smashed through some barriers quickly. Not only did I avoid working the impossible hours lawyers typically put in, but I also actually earned the firm money—something students weren't expected to do. The partners even offered me a job after my year of apprenticeship was over.

But I found my idealism as a budding lawyer challenged by something I noticed all around me: I was surrounded by lawyers who weren't happy. In fact, many who hadn't even hit age forty had become downright miserable. I remember one particular Friday when a lawyer in his thirties came into the firm waving a lottery ticket. "See this ticket?" he said. "If I win this thing, you'll never see my face again."

The strange part is that he owned the firm (and made a big income every year, may I add). It's never a good sign when the owner of a thriving firm buys a lottery ticket, hoping to cash out and leave it all behind.

I used to tell my fellow law school graduates, "If you can find a happy lawyer in this city, I'll pay you a million dollars." I knew it was a safe bet since none of us could find a happy lawyer.

A GNAWING NEGATIVITY

How do people who seemingly have everything end up jaded and disillusioned so quickly? The juxtaposition of sleek office towers, luxury cars, tailored suits, and expensive lunches coupled with chronic dissatisfaction still surprises me. But it shouldn't.

Jesus told us it was very possible, even *probable,* that we could gain the world and lose our soul.[1] I get that. But in the trenches of success, I saw more than a happiness deficit in the people around me. I saw a much deeper and more pervasive condition: cynicism. I often wondered, *How do you go from idealistic to cynical in just a few short years?*

It's a troubling question, and over the years I've asked it again and again. Chances are you've seen it happen around you too . . .

- Your friend who has had her heart broken many times now thinks no man can be trusted.
- Your optimistic college roommate who went into investment banking is convinced all his colleagues are simply in it for themselves, which is exactly why he is now too.
- Your brother-in-law cop has seen too much too many times to believe the best about anybody anymore.
- Even your teammate at work shoots down every idea you bring to the table, instantly listing the many reasons your strategy is doomed to fail.

The people around you can be depressing. But almost as disturbing as what we see *around* us is what we feel *within* us. Cynicism isn't just something other people experience; it's something you sense growing within you. While the time line may vary given your life experience, here's what many people discover: the optimism of your teens and twenties gives way to the realism of your thirties. By the time you hit thirty, many of your once-in-love friends have split up, many of your once-enthusiastic coworkers hate their jobs, and many once-solid friendships have dissolved.

So where does the realism of your thirties lead? That depends. Unchecked, it could lead you into the abyss that is cynicism.

SINKHOLE AHEAD

I remember the first time I saw cynicism begin to grow within me. I was in my early thirties. Paradoxically, it was in pastoral ministry and not the practice of law that I felt cynicism begin to take root in my heart. Halfway through law school, I sensed God calling me into full-time ministry of some kind. I had grown up in a Christian home, and after drifting in my late teen years, I recommitted my life to Christ in my early twenties. Despite my renewed Christianity, though, law was my main focus. I never imagined leaving law to pursue preaching or congregational ministry. But that's the amazing thing about feeling called to something: we're taken in a new direction on an unexpected adventure.

After sensing God calling me into ministry, I took a few years to figure out exactly what that meant. In the meantime, I finished law school and completed the grueling bar admissions course. After passing the bar exam and earning my license to practice law, I shocked everyone (including myself) by heading off to seminary, purely out of obedience.

Confused about what to do next, I decided to dip my toe into congregational ministry for the first time when I was halfway through seminary. I moved with my wife and young son an hour north of Toronto to a rural community, Oro-Medonte, to begin ministry in the community in which I still live today. My assignment was to serve three small churches that hadn't hired a full-time pastor or grown at all in more than forty years. They called me their "student pastor." That didn't mean I served students; it meant I served the churches as the senior pastor while still a student. It also meant the pay was half what they would pay a "real" minister. But it sounded like a call to me.

The churches were tiny. One had an average attendance of six on Sunday mornings. That included slow-moving vehicles and low-flying aircraft. When my wife, son, and I arrived, we grew the church by 50 percent overnight. It was sensational. The second of the three churches had fourteen people in church most Sundays. And the "megachurch" among the three congregations had an average attendance of twenty-three.

Naturally, when you're in congregations that small, ministry is inherently relational. You visit people and invest in them, all the while trying to unite them around a bigger vision and better strategy that will move the mission forward. Even as our churches grew into the hundreds, I did my best to stay relationally connected. In the first decade of ministry, I was in people's homes almost every day. It was tremendously exciting as more and more new people began to show up.

I still remember the first time a couple I'll call Roger and Mary walked in the door one Sunday morning. It didn't take long to figure out that Roger and Mary had very real needs. They didn't have much money. Their subcompact car constantly broke down. They seemed to go from crisis to crisis in every area of their lives: financial, relational, emotional, and spiritual.

Despite being busy now leading hundreds of people, I decided I would help in every way I could. Even though our church had a small budget, we managed to buy Roger and Mary groceries and gift cards. We gave them gas money and made sure their car stayed on the road. I went to their apartment in the south end of town (a twenty-minute drive each way) to regularly pray with them, encourage them, and help them as much as I could.

Roger and Mary kept asking for more assistance. Their phone calls became more frequent, and I often headed over in the evenings to help them navigate whatever crisis they were facing. I poured my heart and soul into praying for their family and trying to assist them in any way possible. It's not an exaggeration to say I spent more time with their family than I spent with any other family in my first ten years of leadership.

Meanwhile, the little churches grew quickly. More and more people began showing up, and that meant it was difficult to visit people as often as I had previously. There were just too many people. Even as the churches grew, Roger and Mary demanded my personal attention. They were poor, and I knew of God's particular emphasis on caring for the poor. In the midst of it all, I noticed a growing ingratitude and increasing neediness from this couple. At times, helping them felt like trying to empty the ocean with a spoon, but I was determined to serve and demonstrate God's grace.

Before long, Roger and Mary started to bring their two-year-old niece to church with them. She was a great kid, but discipline wasn't a strong skill in the family. Their niece spent time one Sunday running up and down the aisles during church, angering some older members.

The issue came up at one of our elder board meetings. Some members insisted we had to do something about this child who was disrupting the service. I stood up for Roger and Mary's family, telling the board I'd rather have a church full of unruly kids than a church full of well-behaved senior citizens. Fortunately for everyone, that settled the matter. And I told Roger and Mary that it wouldn't be a problem anymore.

Even with that controversy put to rest, this couple seemed to become less and less comfortable as the church continued to grow. Finally one Sunday morning, Roger grabbed his niece and ran out of the church, announcing, "This place isn't for us anymore. You don't care about us! We're leaving!"

I was stunned. Naturally, I followed up with him and asked what on earth had happened.

"You haven't done enough for us," he said.

I had no idea what to say. *Seriously? We haven't done enough? Are you kidding me?*

His comments cut directly and deeply into my small but growing pastoral heart.

"Roger," I mustered, "that breaks my heart. It's not an exaggeration to say that in my time in leadership, I have never spent more one-on-one time with anyone than you and your family. And it's not just me. This community has sacrificed to be here for you again and again."

My words made zero difference. He kept insisting our efforts weren't enough and that we didn't—that *I* didn't—really care about them. He said our church had let him down, that we'd abandoned his family at their lowest point.

I didn't know how to make the situation better. They didn't want to make it better. Then they left the church for good.

THE SLIDE INTO CYNICISM BEGINS

I was shocked. And angry. And heartbroken. I honestly didn't have a category for what happened.

It was in that moment that I felt cynicism welling up inside me. It's like a voice inside me was saying, *Useless. Everything you invested was a total waste of time and energy. And you know what? If he did that to you, others will too. So don't care like you used to. Don't invest in people like you used to. Don't give of yourself like you used to. People will just use you and reject you in the end anyway. There's no point.*

At the time, I hadn't even heard of writers like John Townsend or Henry

Cloud, who have helped scores of people understand what boundaries are. Nor was I good at spotting potential mental health issues. I genuinely tried to help, and in the end I got genuinely burned.

That's how cynicism starts.

Cynicism begins not because you *don't* care but because you *do* care.

It starts because you poured your heart into something and got little in return. Or maybe you got something in return, but it was the opposite of what you desired. You fell in love, only to have that relationship dissolve. You threw your heart into your job, only to be told you were being let go. You were completely there for your mom, only to have her tell you you're such a disappointment.

And you can't help but think to yourself, *What gives?*

Most cynics are former optimists. You'd never know it now, but there was a time when they were hopeful, enthusiastic, and even cheerful. There's something inside the human spirit that wants to hope, wants to think things will get better. Nearly everyone starts life with a positive outlook.

So what happens? How do you go from being so positive to so negative? At least three things happen to the human heart as it grows cynical.

1. You Know Too Much

You would think knowledge is always a good thing. But strangely, knowledge will often sadden you. Solomon, whom we'll meet again later, was world renowned for his wisdom. He put it this way: "The greater my wisdom, the greater my grief. To increase knowledge only increases sorrow."[2] Not exactly the most inspirational thing you've ever read. It's like Eeyore wrote that part of the Bible. While that verse may make for a terrible social media post, the insight itself is quite helpful.

In some ways, ignorance is bliss. Had I never known that some people, like Roger and Mary, would end up being disappointed even after a massive investment by a community of people, it would have been easy—even automatic—to keep investing in people. But having been burned, I found that over the months and years that followed, I began to view needy people more suspiciously. Would they treat me the same way? Would they simply walk away too?

Chances are you've had a Roger and Mary in your life. Or four. Or six. So trust becomes harder because you know too much. If your heart hadn't been broken a dozen times by different people, you would have found it easy to keep dating. If your business partner hadn't sold you out and gutted the company, you might still be an entrepreneur. If your neighbors hadn't been so difficult, you might never have wanted to build a fence.

But now you know too much. You've experienced the heartbreak, betrayals, and backstabbing. You understand that people let you down. You've seen that some people can't be trusted. You know love hurts. You realize that people are fickle and selfish. You recognize that not everyone succeeds, despite good intentions and best efforts. The longer you live, the more you know. Which is why cynicism and age are frequent companions.

Why would Solomon link more knowledge with more grief? Because that's the way life works. Knowledge often brings sorrow because the more you know, the more you see life for what it *really* is.

I don't intend to depress you, but let's be honest: life isn't easy; it's a struggle, filled with disappointments and setbacks. Look around long enough and you'll see heartbreak everywhere. You'll see fallibility and frailty. You'll see scheming and manipulation. You'll recognize the power plays and the selfish pursuits that make up so much of human existence.

In fact, the more successful you become, the more pain you're likely to experience. Just ask the lawyers in Toronto or most people who are successful. Just ask Solomon. Ecclesiastes is a cynic's guide to the universe. There's a gnawing hollowness that comes with success. And there's a desperate brokenness that comes from doing life with flawed people.

Don't worry. Hope is coming. But just linger here a little longer to understand why so many cynics struggle with life. Knowledge does bring sorrow. You see life for what it truly is, and it's . . . lacking.

2. You Project the Past onto the Future

Cynicism grows beyond its infancy when you start to protect yourself from future hurt. Having been burned once or twice, you tell yourself only fools get burned three times. So you start to guard your heart. You shelter your soul.

But what starts as self-preservation soon morphs into something more insidious. You become a bit jaded. You're a little wiser, you tell yourself, but look closer and you'll see a different reality. What you have is not wisdom as much as hurt and fear forming calluses around your heart.

In fact, sharp as you are, you begin to look for patterns. And to your surprise, you spot them. Many people are untrustworthy. Maybe the answer isn't joining another company, because no one seems happy at that place either. And you realize the pain of disappointment runs through many of your friends' marriages as deeply as it runs through yours.

With age and experience, you become skilled at seeing patterns. You start to do what cynics do by instinct: you project past failures onto new situations. You meet a new couple and suspect they'll take advantage of you like Roger and Mary did. Better not get too close. You get a new boss and assume she's probably as unfair and arrogant as your old boss. A guy transfers to your team at work, and you're sure it's just a matter of time until he screws up. Your cousin gets married, and you wonder how long it will be before the newlyweds run into serious problems.

You no longer see people for who they are. You no longer see situations for what they could be. You just see potential hurt. Past pain will become future hurt if you let it. So you don't let it.

That became my reality. Because it wasn't just Roger and Mary who caused me pain. There were others, including friends. In fact, what gave birth to my most cynical phase of life (in my thirties) was a series of events that came within a few years of one another.

Roger and Mary weren't the only ones who left. As we implemented a radical set of changes at the churches, more people walked away. Men and women I thought were on board with us for life, in fact, weren't. Even though our churches were adding people faster than we were losing them, it didn't make up for the disappointment I felt.

Within the first few years of our ministry, a set of close friendships also imploded on us. These were the kind of friends you do life with: concerts, dinners, holidays. I was their pastor and they attended our church, but we were still incredible friends. But for some strange reason, within the span of a year, these friends stopped going to our church, and before long, they weren't our friends anymore.

It hurt. Deeply. And I'm still a little confused as to how it all went down. Attempts to make things right didn't work. I know I had a role in the painful situation, but it's all a bit mysterious and murky. And it led me to decide (for a season) to go down the road every cynic travels.

I'm pretty sure you can relate because something similar has happened to you. Eventually, the wariness makes you weary. Your guardedness and suspicion evolve into anger and bitterness.

3. You Decide to Stop Trusting, Hoping, and Believing

After those friendships dissolved, I told Toni, "I don't need friends. Really. Friends were a bad idea. I'm fine on my own." Dumb, I know. But that was my pain speaking. And at the time, it made perfect sense. In fact, it was far safer than the risks new friendships would involve. It's rarely the first round of anguish that breaks your heart permanently. For me, a few previous friendships had also faded over the years, and eventually I questioned whether people were worth the bother. At times I even wondered if I had some fatal flaw embedded in my personality that doomed friendship.

The problem with generalizing—applying one particular situation to *all* situations—is that the death of trust, hope, and belief is like a virus, infecting everything. You think you're protecting yourself from the future when, in reality, your new stance infects your present. The people you care about most in the here and now suffer. That's because as a cynic, you project your newfound suspicion on everyone and everything. Your current relationships stall out or dial back a few notches. The withdrawal isn't just from the future; you retreat from the present as well.

So you become numb to the people you claim to love most, even your spouse and kids. You find yourself predicting cynical endings to moments that used to fill you with joy. You might also find yourself becoming jaded at work. You don't really want to get to know the new guy because, well, you already know what he's like. And the projects and goals that used to motivate and excite you? They just don't anymore.

Perhaps most disturbingly, cynicism begins to infect your relationship with God. When you close your heart to people, you close your heart to God. That shouldn't surprise us, but it does. It only makes sense that the very act of hardening your heart to people simply hardens your heart. And that's the danger—when you close yourself off to people, you close yourself off to God. You find yourself trusting less and doubting more. When you read through Scripture, you want to put an asterisk beside all the promises you read, convincing yourself they don't apply to you. Even your prayer life becomes stunted. What's the point of it anyway? You feel like you're praying for things that won't happen, so why bother?

It's a stifling progression: from knowing too much, to projecting the past onto the future, to snuffing out trust, hope, and belief. But when this process occurs, you have the unmistakable ingredients for cynicism. And whether you're twenty-three or sixty-three, it's a sad—and unnecessary—way to live.

WHY DOES ANY OF THIS MATTER?

Have you ever noticed there are very few "balanced" elderly people? You know how when you're in your twenties or thirties, you still have good days and bad days? You have your ups and downs, but things tend to even out over the long haul. Well, I've noticed that this pattern seems to go away when people reach a certain age.

Most of the older people I know have landed on one side or the other of the balance line. They have grown to be either happy and grateful or bitter and crotchety. It's like you reach an age when a magnet pulls you off the centerline and lands you on the happiness side or the misery side of life. The "I'm having a bad day" feeling we sometimes experience early in life morphs into an "I'm having a bad life" feeling by age seventy. Why is that?

My theory goes like this: As you grow older, you become more of who you already are. Just like your body stiffens a bit, your personality becomes less flexible. It's like there's this war inside you that's battling for hope—and cynicism will win, or it will lose. But you won't just be a little cynical or a little hopeful. The die is cast, and the concrete hardens.

I felt this dynamic intensely throughout my forties. It was like a battle for my soul was going on. I finally began to understand how people grow cynical, jaded, and coldhearted. I had all of that lodged within me. Hope hadn't died, but cynicism was threatening to snuff it out. I realized it would be easy to let despair win. Actually, I realized that left unchecked, cynicism *would* win.

What I needed to understand is what you need to understand: cynicism is actually a choice. Cynics aren't born; they're made. Life doesn't make you a cynic; *you* make you a cynic.

Cynicism is not always a *conscious* decision, but it's a decision nonetheless. It's the decision you make to stop hoping, trusting, and believing. But think about what's at stake. Cynics never change the world. They just tell you why the world can't change. Ask them; they know all about it. And that's where I knew I would end up unless I changed course.

If you've grown cynical, please understand that cynicism happens not because your heart is closed but because it was once open. It happens because the idealist in you was idealistic. And then life happened. All the hurt happened. Now you're left with a choice. So what do you do?

Of course, the cynic might say there's nothing to be done. This is just a natural state of affairs after having been burned in life. It's not difficult to agree with the philosophers who conclude that life is nasty, brutish, and short[3] and with others who insist that hell is other people.[4]

Sadly, that's where too many people leave the conversation. Cynicism is not inevitable. And even once you become a cynic, you don't have to stay a cynic. There is a path back. It's a path for those who are brave and those who long to hope again. Cynicism has an antidote. The question is, Are you willing to embrace it?

2

KICKING CYNICISM
IN THE TEETH

Practical Ways to Defeat Your Inner Cynic

One afternoon a few years ago, I was surfing through TV channels when I saw a professor being interviewed on PBS. To me, it was an amazing interview. This man was a legit prof: tweed jacket, bow tie, and spectacles (spectacles, not glasses, because he was that kind of professor). He sat up straight in his chair, his eyes sparkling. There was even a lilt in his voice. He said things like "What we're discovering is . . ." and "Current theories suggest. . . ." The part that struck me most was his age; he was about eighty years old. *Eighty.* I remember thinking, *Whatever it takes to be that fresh and alive at eighty, I'll do it.* I could feel the battle with cynicism waging inside me, and it was clear that cynicism hadn't won in the life of that elderly professor. However that happened, I wanted it.

Cynicism is so cruel. When I was at my most cynical, the thing that died within me was hope—hope that the future would be better than the past, hope that the next time could be different, hope that my heart would feel again. And that leads us to the ultimate antidote for cynicism, which happens to be the foundation for the Christian faith: hope. Cynics find hope hard because hope is one of cynicism's first casualties. The concept of hope is a thread that runs through the scriptural narrative and is at the epicenter of what people call the gospel (literally, "good news").

Sometimes people struggle with the Bible and Christianity because it's so *real*. How can Christianity be founded on hope when so much of the story is violent, oppressive, and bleak? I mean, have you ever read the Bible? It contains plenty of tragedy, trauma, and treachery. You might think that flipping through biblical stories would make you *more* cynical, not less cynical.

When one of my boys was little, his favorite Bible story featured Samson and Delilah. I started to get nervous when he asked me to read it night after night. After all, the story has almost no redeeming qualities. God gives a man a gift of strength, and the man falls madly in love, stupidly squanders his gift, and gives the secret away . . . lying through his teeth all the while. Then he goes out with a bang, killing thousands of people and himself in one spectacular feat of brute strength as he demolishes a temple. And nobody lived happily ever after. Amen.

For years, it bothered me that Scripture has so many violent accounts. In some instances, it still bothers me. But it also made me realize something far more profound than I would normally see through my sanitized, twenty-first-century, middle-class, Western mind-set: God understands our world. He understands how brutal we often are and how awful human nature can be. God sees how violent we can be toward one another and toward ourselves. He sees our cruelty. Without God's intervention in the narrative of the human story, life would be nasty, brutish, and short.

Instead of letting our inhumanity be the final word, God entered the mess in human form through Jesus and conquered hate with love. We threw the worst of humanity directly at Jesus: hatred, abuse, ridicule, rejection, and death. And God turned it into life. And not just life for himself but also life for *us,* for humanity, for the very people who killed his Son.

The cynics thought they were winning on the last Thursday of Jesus's life. They were certain they had the final word on Friday. They were in control. Despair had won. Even the disciples thought so. They went home, back to fishing. But nobody saw Sunday coming. Nobody saw hope rising. No one saw love breaking out from the ashes of hate. Nobody saw Jesus coming back.

The remarkable part of Christianity is not that we have a Savior who came to deliver us but that we have a Savior who sees us for who we really are and loves us anyway. Jesus stared hate in the face and met it with love. He confronted despair and made it abundantly clear it wouldn't win.

The thrust of the gospel is that Jesus sees *your* hate and meets it with love. He sees *your* despair and counters it with hope. He sees *your* doubt and lobs belief back at you again and again. Cynicism melts under the relentless hope of the gospel.

Your past isn't your future. Not if you get Jesus involved.

Bitterness can't linger under the relentless assault of love.

Hope cannot die if an empty tomb empowers it.

Of all people on earth, Christians should be the least cynical. After all, the gospel gives us the greatest reasons to hope. We don't just cling to an intellectual claim or proposition. Our hope isn't based on an emotion or a feeling. It lives in a person who beat death itself and who loves us deeply enough to literally go through hell to rescue us. So what were you discouraged about again?

Because hope is anchored in resurrection, it is resilient. It can withstand a thousand Rogers and Marys. It can outlast a dozen or a hundred frustrating jobs. It can outmaneuver ten thousand broken hearts. If you want to kick cynicism in the teeth, trust again. Hope again. Believe again. That's the hope found in Jesus Christ. And that, in the end, is what defeats cynicism.

AND NOW A LITTLE TRICK

As true as the hope of Christ is, remembering it can be difficult in the grind of everyday life. At least it can be for me when my eyes start to roll and my heart starts to harden . . . again. And if the answer to the rise of cynicism is the gospel, isn't that kind of like saying Jesus is the answer to every question? Hey, ultimately, I think Jesus is the answer, but still, sometimes it's good to get more granular. So *how* is Jesus the answer? *How* do you battle cynicism on the days when discouragement and despair are once again knocking at your door? That brings me to the little hack I've picked up to help me in the times I struggle to battle my creeping cynicism. An incredibly effective antidote to cynicism is *curiosity*. Yes, simple curiosity.

One thing I've noticed again and again is this reality: curious people are never cynical, and cynical people are never curious. That's what amazed me about the professor on PBS that afternoon. He may have been eighty, but he was *curious*. He was still exploring, still thinking, still open, still wondering. He was still fully alive.

Think for a minute about the wonderfully curious people you know: a friend, a former teacher, a neighbor, or an uncle. You'll quickly realize that the curious are always interested, always hopeful, and always open to new possibilities. Some grandparents are infinitely interested in their children and grandchildren, asking questions, discovering new things together, embracing the changing possibilities of a new world. Some have more joy for tomorrow than they did decades earlier and become cheerleaders for hope in their communities, families, and congregations.

How to Cultivate Curiosity

If curiosity is the discipline that kills cynicism and keeps hope alive, how do you become more curious? Like most things, curiosity is a habit that can be nurtured and developed. Feed your curiosity, and it grows. Starve it, and it withers.

Here are five keys I've discovered to help anyone become more curious and stay curious throughout life.

1. Schedule Thinking Time

Busyness is the enemy of wonder, and many people feel frantically busy these days. Think about it: When was the last time you felt curious while you were in a hurry? Curiosity needs time to breathe and explore. Hurry, in contrast, looks for shortcuts. Worse, it cuts people off. It asks for a summary or synopsis, not a fully developed story or explanation.

So schedule time to ponder and process. Write it in your calendar. Then pick up a book on a subject you know nothing about and start reading. Or go for coffee with a friend and ask a dozen really good questions. Or Google something until your brain fires up a whole new sequence of neurons.

Take it even further. Go for a hike, a long walk, a run, or a bike ride. So many people discover their best thinking time happens when they're doing something physical, whether that's a five-mile run or something as simple as raking leaves. Schedule some wide-open space in your calendar and let your mind take you to new places. You can't wonder and discover when you're in a hurry.

2. Ask Open-Ended Questions

Later on, we'll talk about the death of conversation in our culture and how it's making us more disconnected than ever. At the heart of conversation's demise is a lack of question asking.

The discipline of asking questions is healthy and helpful for many reasons, one being that questions spark curiosity. The curious go into the deep end of question asking by asking a particular kind: they ask *open-ended* questions.

Too often in our culture, questions serve as a way of getting to a predetermined point. As a lawyer, I was trained in question asking and cross-examination. Too much conversation these days is designed to extract information and move on, just like a lawyer would. Narrow question asking is a sign you're not genuinely interested in the answer or the person.

If I'm not careful, I formulate my next question or comment as the other person is speaking. As soon as it seems as if the response is wrapping up, I feel like I need to jump in. Ever done that? Yeah, that's a bad move.

The curious ask broad, probing questions—and then sit back and listen. Next time, when it sounds like the other person is finishing an answer, just wait. You'll be surprised at where that leads. Many people will offer more. I can't tell you how often that's led to pure-gold insight and conversation. If you listen longer than most people listen, you'll hear things most people never hear.

3. Give Fewer Answers

In addition to being skilled at asking broad questions, the curious also try to refrain from always giving an answer. If you need to be the authority on everything, you'll kill conversation. Even when curious people have an answer or a response to a question, they'll often volley back with a question that goes something like "Those are my thoughts, but what do *you* think?" And like a good game of tennis, the rally continues.

Giving fewer answers not only affects the person you're talking to, but it also has an impact on you. Do it long enough, and you'll find that the restraint makes you challenge your own thinking, causes you to ask yourself more questions, and encourages you to dig deeper.

If you're worried that people won't find you as convincing as you used to be, relax. Most people will find you *more* persuasive and compelling. Openness attracts people and draws them in. Increasingly in our culture, certainty is off-putting.

4. Dream More

Remember when you used to dream? What happened to that? Most adults want more control over their lives. Control is about certainty; it's about the known. When your life becomes focused on what you know and what you can control, dreams die.

You start to settle for the probable, not the possible. Curious people dream. They wonder. They imagine. If you spend more time dreaming, you'll find your cynicism fades.

5. Ask Two Pivotal Questions

Finally, the curious come back to two questions again and again: "Why?" and "Why not?"

"Why?" is at the heart of curiosity. Asking "Why?" consistently is the reason you were so annoying to your mother when you were six, incessantly repeating the question until you were shushed into silence. You were trying to figure out the world and carried so few assumptions into it. What a magical time.

Maybe it's time to resurrect "Why?" Why is the sky blue? Why does gravity make people stick to the planet? Why do birds fly? Why is your best friend feeling discouraged? Why do politicians behave the way they do? Why do people feel the emotions they do?

To foster curiosity, also ask, "Why not?" Why not do it differently? Why not say yes? Why not try it? Why not try a new way? Widen your universe when other people seem to be narrowing theirs.

The curious ask, "Why?" And they ask, "Why not?" Try it.

CYNICISM DOESN'T STAND A CHANCE

That list is hardly exhaustive. You can expand it, but you see its potential, don't you?

Curiosity is a discipline, and it's a viewpoint. If you can adopt a curious outlook day after day, you will discover that cynicism never gets a toehold. Remember, the cynics are never curious, and the curious are never cynical.

You will also discover that the full power of the gospel gets a firm foothold in the lives of the curious. You won't automatically discount the promises of Scripture. You'll lose the asterisk that says none of this applies to you. You'll pray and actually begin to believe there's a God in heaven who hears you. You'll realize that tomorrow can be different from today, and you'll affirm the promise that anyone who is in Christ is a new creation.

Imagine yourself at eighty. What's happened to you in the decades between today and then? Has your heart grown? Has it hardened? Is your mind flourishing, or have you shut it down? Are you alive and filled with wonder? Or did your passion die decades ago? That's what's at stake.

So hope again. Believe again. Trust again. And be curious. Cultivate curiosity long enough, and hope will flourish. And when hope flourishes, cynicism doesn't stand a chance.

PART II

COMPROMISE

3

SUCCESSFUL
(ON THE OUTSIDE)

Why Character Determines Your True Capacity

I can't say I experience supernatural occurrences very often. I can count on two hands the number of times I'm *pretty sure* I heard from God directly. I don't need my toes for that equation yet, even though I'm a pastor. For the most part, I sense that I hear from God when I read the Bible and get specific advice from godly people.

A handful of times, however, I've felt like God directly intervened in my life. I realize some people don't believe God ever speaks to us. I respect that. I know other people view divine intervention as a sign of spiritual maturity ("Wow, you heard from *God*? You must be *so up there* spiritually."). Personally, I think hearing directly from God can be a sign of spiritual *immaturity* more than maturity, meaning God had to intervene in my life supernaturally because I was too dumb or insensitive to get the message any other way.

Regardless of what you believe about supernatural events, it's about the only way I know how to explain what happened to me in my first summer as a law intern. I had one of those surreal moments the summer after my first year of law school. I was working at my first job in a law firm in my hometown. I had known the senior partner since I was a kid. I wanted to work at his firm because I knew he shared the same faith I did, and I wanted to make sure I could practice law in an ethical setting. Ethics were important both to me and to him.

As far as I was concerned, the firm was passing the test. By the time August rolled around, I had been there three months, and they had already indicated they would invite me back to practice there when I graduated. Things were going great.

But one afternoon in late summer, I had an experience the likes of which I'd never had before. It changed my life. I was in the office of one of the partners, standing behind his desk, working on a file. He was gone for the day and had given me permission to use his office, which beat the space I usually occupied. As I was looking up from the desk to think through my strategy on a particular case, I had a vision. I call it a vision because I don't know how else to describe it. I was wide awake, but I saw a clear picture of myself twenty years in the future. In that vision, I was forty-four years old and enjoyed a thriving law practice. I was extremely successful . . . but also morally bankrupt. My marriage and family had fallen apart. My values were compromised. And I wasn't anything like the person I thought I was going to be, despite my outward success.

I knew in an instant that the vision meant I wasn't going to practice law. I don't know why I knew that, but sometimes you're just certain about things. And in that moment, I felt certain.

The vision was disarming to say the least, and other than sensing that law was not for me, it left me more confused than anything. After all, I had wanted to be a lawyer since I was eight years old, and by every indication, I was good at it. Now my whole life plan had been blown to bits in an instant.

I left the partner's office and headed down the hallway to the boardroom to put some books away. The boardroom had a big bay window, which I stared out, wondering what all of this might mean. I started praying about it because I wanted to find and follow God's plan for my life. I then felt a prompting that told me to look down the street.

ARE YOU KIDDING ME?

As I looked down First Street, I saw the church I grew up in, but the only part of the building I could see from the law office was the window of the pastor's office. The next thing I heard inside my spirit was *You should be in there.*

That was the beginning of two things. It was the first time I ever sensed a call to ministry. To say it left me stunned would be an understatement. I had *never* entertained the thought of ministry before. There were a thousand reasons it made no sense. I don't have the gift set pastors typically have, plus I had always felt sorry for pastors (couldn't they get a real job somewhere?). But what I experienced that day was unmistakable in my mind.

Things became even clearer when I picked up my soon-to-be fiancée after work. With my head still spinning as I drove her to my parents' house for dinner, Toni asked, "Have you ever thought about going into ministry?" We had never once talked about that before. My response? "You'll never guess what happened to me at the office today." That started a conversation that changed our lives forever.

That's probably enough meaning to pull from one experience. But there was more. Much more. The second thing that vision did was alert me to a tension almost every person feels at some point: the potential disconnect between who you are and who you know you should be. That pull has been constant in my life, even in ministry. You would think that being in ministry would inoculate me from moral compromise. It doesn't. All of us can cheat our values anywhere.

I now believe that vision was as much about life as it was about law, giving me a deep glimpse into the battle over character that every one of us fights. Far too many of us end up compromised: who we are no longer lines up with who we had hoped to be. And it happens so subtly that most of the time we don't even know it's going on.

The Subtle Art of Selling Your Soul

Most of us know people who have sold out, who've given in to the dark forces of greed, self-absorption, blind ambition, moral trade-offs, or ruthlessness. In the process, they threw integrity out the window. And even if you don't personally know someone who's done this, a quick scan of the headlines on any given day will usually yield an athlete, a politician, or a business leader who has.

So how does a person get there? How does one end up like my vision of myself at forty-four, successful on the outside but corroded on the inside? Even if your family hasn't forsaken you and it hasn't cost you your job, you may sometimes look in the mirror with the sinking feeling that you didn't do what you should have done and you're not who you thought you'd be.

There was that time when you weren't 100 percent honest with a client, or maybe many clients. You could have kept the promise, but you didn't. You haven't told your wife about your porn problem, but you tell yourself it's no big deal when you know deep down it's ruining your intimacy with her. You know you should be more present for your kids, but you hide behind your laptop because you just can't handle the chaos of bedtime and don't want yet another fight with your wife. Work is just easier. At least people respect you there.

You flirted with someone when your husband wasn't looking—not a lot, but just enough to get a glance back that told you he found you attractive and desirable. And it made you feel better than it should have. You used to look down on women who took a third glass of wine, but now the pressure you feel juggling all the demands on you makes three drinks seem like no big deal. And sure, you talk about your friend behind her back in a way you never would to her face, but doesn't everyone?

The subtle compromises we make day after day—the half truths, the rationalizations, the excuses—create a gap between who we are and who we want to be. You're not a terrible person, but you're certainly not at your best either. And if you got dead honest with yourself, you'd say that although you haven't sold your soul to the devil, you've rented it.

A thousand little compromises have left you . . . compromised.

COMPETENCY ISN'T EVERYTHING IT'S CRACKED UP TO BE

As a young leader, I was convinced that competency was the key to success in life. My formula went like this: Competency determines capacity. The more competent you are, the greater your potential. The greater your potential, the greater your capacity. As a driven kind of person, I was motivated by that. Keep learning, hone your craft, sharpen your mind, find a great mentor, and spend hundreds—maybe thousands—of hours developing yourself, and you will realize your potential. The only real limit to your capacity is your competency.

So I read books. I got my education. I went to conferences. I networked. I enlisted mentors and hired coaches. I just wanted to be the best. I took a deep dive into the assumption that competency was the key to advancement. Be the smartest person in the room, sharpen your skill set, and all will be well.

But a few years into my adult life, I began to notice highly competent people who became disqualified from leadership. These were smart, skilled people with great educations, incredible minds, and finely tuned skill sets who were at the top of their fields. One after another, they resigned or were forced out.

These people usually left their esteemed positions because of an addiction, an affair, abuse, embezzlement, greed, internal fighting, ego, or sometimes just being a jerk. Athletes, politicians, business leaders, actors, industry moguls, and pastors alike fall to issues like these month after month, year after year, decade after decade. And those are only the ones we hear about. Start looking for the stories that never make the news, and the onslaught seems endless.

Seeing all this around me, I began to rethink my theory. What if competency doesn't determine capacity? If it's true that your capacity functions as your ability to contribute to life—to make a difference—then clearly, competency is not the lid, as demonstrated in case after case, story after story. Highly competent people get taken out day after day. And even if they don't get taken out, their potential is still capped.

So if competency doesn't determine capacity, what does?

Character does. All the competency in the world can't compensate for a lack of character. Ultimately, your character is your lid. Even in a workplace that wouldn't espouse any religious affiliation at all, character is the great leveler. You may be smart, but if people don't like you, they won't want to work with you. You may be the best software developer in your field, but if you lie, people won't trust you. You may be able to bring reams of cash into the company, but if you mistreat the people who work with you, they'll leave or they'll make sure you do.

Lack of character kills careers, shatters families, ruins friendships, and destroys influence. And even if you never get fired or divorced over the compromises you make, your lack of character will limit the intimacy, joy, and depth you experience with God and with people.

Like it or not, *character,* not competency, determines capacity.

SO CHARACTER IS EVERYTHING . . . REALLY?

Character determines so much more than you think. Ultimately, it not only dictates your capacity in work and in life but also becomes your legacy. Your competency leaves the first impression, but your character leaves the lasting one. The crowd is intrigued by your competency, but your family and close friends are influenced by your character.

Still not convinced? Years ago, Stephen Covey encouraged all of us to think about our funerals.[1] I'd like to encourage you to do the same thing. Think about who will attend your funeral; at the very center of the gathering will be your spouse, your kids, your remaining siblings and other family members, and a few close friends.

As a pastor, I've done my share of funerals over the years. In over two decades of helping families after a death, I've never seen a son pull out his dad's résumé at the funeral. I've never heard the kids discuss a parent's net worth while they stood around the casket or urn. I promise you, nobody close to you will be reciting the stats from your final quarter at your celebration of life.

When I meet with families after a death, the legacy of the person who died becomes apparent within minutes. Sadly, it's not always great. I've seen some very hurt spouses and kids try to find nice things to say but come up with only a few awkward phrases that mask years of pain. I've also seen hearts that over time have grown dull and even indifferent to the deceased. Sure, nobody's *glad* she's dead, but they're not necessarily sad either.

It may be sobering to know that this actually happens, but it does. Any eulogy you hear is a "best of" litany or a "highlight reel" from the life story, but sometimes the speech is short for a reason. When you're no longer breathing, the legacy you'll leave will center on your character. People will remember if you loved well, if you forgave easily, if you cared enough to be there for them. They'll remember if you served or preferred to be served. They'll know whether you thought life revolved around you or whether you really tried to honor God and others. They'll remember whether you were generous or miserly, arrogant or humble, compassionate or indifferent. They'll remember your temper or whether you learned the rhythms of grace.

To be honest, I'm a little nervous about what people would say if I died right now. I think I'm more of a mixed bag than I am anything else. Thankfully, this is not yet the end of my story or your story. If you think it's too late, it's not. The final chapter in your life isn't written. Before you grow too despondent over your past, remember that your family will also remember your *progress*. Which means you should never give up.

I can't tell you how many times I've heard adult children say things like "When I was younger, Dad had a terrible temper. But he changed a lot. He's been so much kinder over the last few years." Or "Mom and Dad used to fight every day. But it's so great to see how they've learned to honor and respect each other over the last few decades." I've also heard variations on "Dad used to work all the time [or drink all the time or ignore us all the time], but as we've gotten older, he's changed. And you should have seen him with the grandkids. They adored him."

Perhaps the hardest part is that eventually your life and mine will get reduced to a single sentence. Not in the first weeks or months after our passing. But give it a year or so, and all of us will be described by a single sentence: "My mom? She was such a kind person. We miss her. Hey, what's for dinner?" Or "My dad worked a lot, and he sure loved his Corvette. What time's the game on?"

Sobering, isn't it?

This book alone is over fifty thousand words long, and it's not my only book. I will have lived at least five decades by the time I die (hopefully many more), had thousands of conversations, met thousands of people, and spoken to thousands of leaders. But in the end, everyone who knew me well, including my family, will condense my contributions to something like "Oh, Carey, he was _____. Can you pass the salsa?"

It's what might fill in the blank that gets me. Not because I care what my reputation will be but because I care about the impact I will have had on the people closest to me. As some leaders have said, "I want the people who know me the best to love me the most." Sadly, often the opposite is true. If you don't nurture your character daily, you can be most admired by the people who know you least, while the people who know you best struggle with you the most.

Fortunately for all of us, it's not over yet. Keep honing your heart. Keep nurturing your soul. You may not be who you want to be, but you're not done yet.

THE STRUGGLE IS REAL

Developing your character is never easy, which is why so many people abandon the pursuit. But it's so worth it. Character matters more than anything because you bring who you are into everything you do. Your character determines the kind of spouse, parent, friend, employee, and leader you are. No matter how hard you try, you can't escape *you*.

So why don't we all have stellar character? Why is it so difficult to be who we had hoped to be? Few people describe the human struggle as honestly or as clearly as a writer did almost two millennia ago. By all accounts, he was an exceptional leader. He helped early Christianity grow from a local gathering of people who believed that Jesus rose from the dead to a global movement, all within a few decades. To say God used Paul is an understatement. No one other than Jesus had greater influence or impact in the first century of Christianity than Paul did.

You would think that Paul had a fantastic interior life, that his prayer life was stellar, that he was rarely tempted to do wrong. Since God used him so powerfully, you would expect that Paul never struggled to be the person God called him to be or to reflect the grace and character of the Savior he worshipped.

Apparently that wasn't the case, and amazingly we have a record of his internal battle:

> I don't really understand myself, for I want to do what is right, but I don't do it. Instead, I do what I hate. . . .
>
> I want to do what is right, but I can't. I want to do what is good, but I don't. I don't want to do what is wrong, but I do it anyway. . . .
>
> I have discovered this principle of life—that when I want to do what is right, I inevitably do what is wrong. I love God's law with all my heart. But there is another power within me that is at war with my mind. This power makes me a slave to the sin that is still within me. Oh, what a miserable person I am![2]

Ever felt like that? It's why your family life isn't quite what you pictured it to be when you were dating, and you know a big part of that problem is you. Ditto with your friendships, which are sometimes so complicated, and you know you're part of the reason why. It's why you struggle at work, where so much of your battle is internal and relational.

If you're still breathing oxygen, then Paul pretty much described the struggle you feel, didn't he? You have ideals, but you live in the real world with real challenges. Despite your best intentions, you compromise enough to leave you compromised.

Signs You're Losing the Battle

How does compromise start? Sometimes it begins intentionally. You know you're cheating. You know you're lying. You took the bait. But often, compromise doesn't begin that way. It happens more subtly.

As Paul admitted, the struggle has an innate quality to it. Compromise is *in* you, and life brings it out of you. You're surrounded by people who compromise, who have made a hundred little concessions. It's not hard to drift. It's not difficult to give in. Go with the flow, and before you know it, you've crossed the line.

So what are some telltale signs you're drifting, that you're not becoming who you intend to be? Here are five.

1. There's a Growing Gap Between Your Public Life and Private Life

Your character is compromised when you can no longer tell the world the truth. You project an image of yourself that isn't accurate. You do a simple and innocent version of this when you have guests to your home for dinner. You mow the lawn, clear the crumbs off the kitchen counter, tell the kids to clean their rooms, pick up the towels off the bathroom floor, and put out fresh flowers. Then you pretend you live like this all the time.

Sprucing up your home for guests is pretty benign, but more serious is when you project to the world an exterior image of who you are that doesn't truly reflect your interior life. Watch for any gap you see between your words and your deeds. When you talk grace, but you snap at your spouse, kids, and staff, that's a gap. When you talk financial responsibility with your colleagues, but your personal finances are a mess, that's a gap.

When you say people matter, but you make zero time for anyone in need, that's a gap.

You hate this kind of gap when you see it in others. You call it hypocrisy, and that's exactly what it is. The English word *hypocrisy* stems from the Greek word for "actor." A hypocrite was an actor who donned a mask to portray a character. That's what hypocrites do: they pretend to be someone they're not.

While it's easy to spot hypocrisy in others, it's much harder to see it in ourselves. That's because we judge ourselves by our *intentions* and other people by their *actions*. It's completely unfair but exceptionally common. You know what you *intended* to do or how you *wish* you had responded. So you cut yourself some slack. Then you put a thin veneer over the action that masks it and makes it look a little more like the intention. And that's the beginning of the disconnect between who you are and who you want to be.

2. You're Hiding Things

As the gap grows between your real self and the projection of your false self, you won't want anyone to discover the truth about you. Compromise eventually leads to cover-up.

Because you realize (even on the subconscious level) that you're not who you should be, you're ashamed to admit what you're doing. You tell the accountant to make some changes in case you get audited. You delete your browser history. You change the password on your phone and tell your spouse that work required it. You fabricate stories to conceal the facts.

Cover-up is almost daily fodder for newspapers because it's so common in business and politics. It's typical in those fields because it's so common everywhere. We all start misleading and misinforming others whenever we feel ashamed of what we've done or who we've become. It's just that most of us never make the news.

3. You Fail to Follow Through on What You've Said

Another sign of compromise is when you commit to things that you never end up doing. That may be a common human condition, but it intensifies as you compromise more and more.

Sure, you say you want to get together with your parents and siblings, but your real priorities have shifted. You promise to meet up soon because that's what decent people say, but you just don't deliver. Similarly, you told your team the report would be done by a certain deadline, but it wasn't. You were just too preoccupied with other things. You promised your spouse a date night, but it never happened because, once again, you got slammed with more urgent matters.

No big deal, you say? If you think your lack of follow-through involves only little things not worthy of a second thought, just know that this is exactly how compromise begins.

4. You Justify Your Bad Actions and Decisions

There's a certain point when you compromise regularly enough that you decide to stop apologizing and instead start justifying. There's a reason you are the way you are.

Everyone in your field behaves the way you do; to change would mean you'd lose. You can't help it that your marriage has grown cold; it happens to all couples. Your irritability is because of the overwhelming pressure you're under; there's nothing you can do about it. And your greed, well, you deserve something good after how hard you've worked; who could fault you for that?

When you start justifying your bad behavior and decisions, you begin to believe your condition is inevitable. You shift blame to circumstances "beyond your control." You convince yourself that if others were in your shoes, they would be just as cynical, unhappy, and compromised as you are. They just don't get it.

5. Your Life Has Become All About You

When you keep compromising, eventually you craft a life that is almost entirely self-centered. And that's the opposite of who you know you should be. Any value system worth having is focused on others, not self. The problem, of course, is that people take time, attention, and love. And you don't have time or energy for that. Not anymore.

If it's all about you, you've done more than rent your soul. Perhaps you've moved into a long-term lease.

NOBODY WILL EVER PAY YOU TO FIX THIS

When you think about how behavioral dynamics work, it's no surprise that compromise is so easy.

First, as Paul so brilliantly chronicled, compromise is a staple of the human condition. We have a natural inclination toward it. Second, pretty much nobody is ever going to ask you to develop your character. Maybe your spouse will, but that's about it. Will other people address it? Maybe, but not from the perspective of encouragement. Instead, they'll just penalize you if you don't. They'll fire you, drop you as a friend, or divorce you. Rarely will anyone encourage you to work on your character proactively.

Contrast that with your competency. People will push you to develop your competency. Your parents likely pushed you to get an education. Competency is so highly valued in our culture that people will often pay you to improve your skill set. Your employer will cover the costs for you to go to a conference or take the training courses you need, or perhaps even fund the tuition for your next degree.

Plus, competency is fun. Who doesn't want to learn a new skill or develop a talent? Devouring a book, listening to a podcast, or taking an online class can be really stimulating. You tend to see tangible results. That skill you picked up is something you can implement this month. That hack you learned has an immediate payoff.

But who's pushing you to be a better *you*? Who's speaking into your life to point out those deep-seated character issues that need to be worked on? Right, cue the silence.

Often, there are only a few people. Worse, maybe there's nobody.

And let's be honest: character development is far more painful than skill development. Working on your character forces you to go into the crags and crevices of your heart. It encourages you to look at your past to forge a better future. It makes you look in the mirror.

When you tackle your character, though, things get uncomfortable. The blaming stops. The excuses get pushed to the side. And honesty— painful honesty—is required. You finally have to deal with you. Which explains why it's so much easier to keep focusing on your competency and keep compromising your character. Character is one of those ethereal concepts that doesn't feel actionable because it seems so airy. But actually that's not true. You can develop your character in the same way you develop a muscle: by exercising it. There are practical disciplines, habits, and patterns that grow character. And that's what we'll look at next.

TAKING YOUR SOUL OFF THE MARKET

Practical Ways to Deepen Your Character

When I was in my late thirties, I went on my first personal retreat. I had been on structured retreats before with spiritual directors, pastors, and professors, but this one was different. I made up all the rules myself. It was just going to be me, disconnected from the world for three days. Think of it as solitary confinement for the soul.

I reasoned that by being alone for three days, I could do soul surgery, boosting my character so much that I'd basically be done for years. And because I was all by myself, I would definitely hear from God.

You know what happened over those three days? I got bored. Fast. Do you have any idea how quiet it is when you shut off your phone, turn off all devices, and sit there alone? Do you know how weird it is to sit in utter silence? It's strange to have nothing on the calendar, no one to talk to, no one to distract you, and nothing to look forward to but a bowl of soup four hours from now. Blaise Pascal was right: "The sole cause of man's unhappiness is that he does not know how to stay quietly in his room."[1]

I expected the retreat to be spiritual growth on steroids. Mostly it was just me sitting by myself, alone, with nothing to do. I prayed, but you run out of things to say over three days. I read my Bible, but I read it every day anyway. I journaled, but how much can you write? I finally gave myself permission to jump online. I gave myself permission to watch sermons because, well, that was spiritual.

Much to my disappointment, nothing profound happened during those three days. No big revelation. There was nothing particularly character building or life changing.

But what I've come to realize is that character development for the most part doesn't happen in some monastery with stone walls and dank cellars. It happens in the grind of everyday life. It has to because that's where your character gets challenged the most: in parking lots, during meetings, amid marital conflict, and at home when you're exhausted and the garbage still needs to be taken out and you trip over the kids' shoes.

I'm all for retreats and will surely do more, but if you don't have a day-to-day strategy, you'll never win the battle for your soul. After watching my character get challenged over the years, I made up a formula that has helped me so much. It's not really math, but if I express it that way, it reminds me of what's really needed.

The antidote to compromise is simply this: work twice as hard on your character as you do on your competency. It could be that you need to work five times harder. Or ten times harder. I don't know. Twice as hard feels doable, and it's a reminder that I'm likely going to resist it, so I'd better pay attention. According to Jesus, very few people ever manage to do it.

SO THERE'S THIS ROAD . . .

Have you ever heard the teaching Jesus gave when he said that "the gateway to life is very narrow and the road is difficult, and only a few ever find it"?[2]

If you have, you've probably heard it explained as though it's about *becoming* a Christian, that very few people ever really trust their lives to Jesus. I understood it that way because that's how I'd heard it taught. I think that's one application, for sure. But I wonder if Jesus had another application in mind, one that shows us how critical character development is and how rare it is. Consider again how he phrased it: "The gateway to life is very narrow and the road is difficult, and only a few ever find it."

If you read this text purely as a commentary on *becoming* a Christian, it's inconsistent with the rest of the New Testament message, which says our salvation doesn't depend on our goodness; our salvation instead depends on trusting our lives to Jesus, who died and rose again to forgive our sins and give us life. After all, becoming a Christian is not about *us* being good; it's about *God* being good to us in Christ. Our response is to trust in Christ.

The context of this teaching provides clues as to what Jesus was talking about. Jesus offered this commentary on the road to life as he was summing up perhaps the greatest sermon ever preached, popularly called the Sermon on the Mount. Even if you don't read the Bible, you may be familiar with Jesus's teachings from that sermon. In those passages, Jesus talked about loving our enemies and not judging people. He even laid down the Golden Rule that you should "do to others whatever you would like them to do to you."[3] The Sermon on the Mount contains some of Jesus's best-known and most-powerful teaching.

Surely, Jesus wasn't saying that *only* if we obey every last bit of the Sermon on the Mount will we enter heaven, as in, "Only a few of you will ever be this righteous, and if you are, welcome to heaven." If that's the case, we're all doomed, me especially.

No, I believe Jesus meant that on the other side of trusting him as Lord, there's a different life—a reshaping of your life—that's found only in completely trusting your character and soul to God. It doesn't save you. Instead, it's a *response* to being saved.

A Different Kind of Invitation

This new life is focused on letting God do the deep work of renewal and regeneration, of making you a new creation. As you let Christ chisel away the stone of your soul, your character, heart, and life get remade into a closer resemblance of God himself. As your character is reshaped from the inside out, your love will flow more deeply. You will stop judging others. You won't look at a woman as an object and lust after her. You won't hate your neighbor. In other words, your life will look much more like the life described in the Sermon on the Mount.

It's almost as though Jesus were saying, "Once you become a follower of mine, we're just getting started. Are you up for the kind of regenerative work I'm ready to do in your life? Are you ready to truly let me remake you from the inside out? I know that the gate to this kind of life is narrow and the road is difficult. I realize few ever find it. But it's so worth it. I'd love you to join me. You in?"

That's a huge invitation and a difficult one to truly embrace. The fact that the transformation Jesus envisions runs so deep and is so painfully personal explains why you meet a lot of Christians who don't look anything like Jesus. And you know the weird part? They probably *are* Christians; they just haven't found the road that leads to life. They still hate. They still judge. They still envy. Because the road to love and life is hard, and the gate is narrow, and few ever find it.

If you do go through the deep journey Jesus invites you to take, you'll stop compromising. Your outside will begin to look like your inside. You won't need to hide because there will be nothing left to hide. You'll be so consistent that there will be no distinction between who you are publicly and who you are privately. Keeping your word will be easy because your yes will mean yes and your no will mean no.

That's what working on your character does. That's what getting your soul back looks like.

Obviously, it's a lifelong journey. The ancients called it sanctification, the process of being made holy, of separating yourself from the things that murder your soul. It's the sometimes-painful work God does in your life, not because he hates you, but because he loves you. Paul knew his internal battle to do what he knew he should do was spiritual, and he believed the solution focused on Christ. Look at how he concluded that honest passage about his struggle: "Who will free me from this life that is dominated by sin and death? Thank God! The answer is in Jesus Christ our Lord."[4]

So how do you begin that reconstruction? How do you reverse the compromises and start working on your character? The process of changing your character from the inside out could fill this entire book, but here are three ways to get started.

1. Take Responsibility

There's a simple reason we blame circumstances and other people rather than own up to our faults and failures: it's easier than dealing with ourselves. Blame is the opposite of responsibility. Every time you blame others, invent justifications, or craft a fresh excuse, you evade responsibility.

Progress begins with self-honesty. When I first started seeing a counselor to deal with some issues Toni and I had in our marriage, I went into his office with a long list of things that were wrong with my wife. A few hours later, I emerged from his office with a long list of things that were wrong with me. It seems strange to pay people to tell you what's wrong with you, but now I see it as a powerful investment in a better future. Guess what happened as soon as I started dealing with *my* issues rather than demanding that Toni deal with her (very few) issues? I started to get better. We also got better, and our marriage got better.

The same dynamic can happen with your character. As soon as you start to admit that you're the problem, you start to make progress. You can blame your team, your board, your spouse, your kids, the economy, your profession, or even gravity, but none of that is going to reshape your character.

If you change everything in your life except your character, you still won't be the kind of person you want to be. You can change jobs. You can change careers. You can change cities. You can change spouses. But none of that changes you.

2. Make Your Talk Match Your Walk

Research shows that the average person hears as many as two hundred lies a day and that "60% of people lie during a typical 10-minute conversation and . . . average two to three lies during that short timeframe."[5] As bad as this sounds, and it is, we're probably not surprised by statistics like this. People tell untruths for many reasons, but almost always it's because they are compromised in some way, to some degree.

A number of years ago, I started watching everything I said publicly to make sure it was actually true. I know that sounds strange, but whenever there's a gap between who you are and who you want to be, your words drift toward exaggeration and embellishment.

For example, I might have been tempted to say I could get a project done when, in reality, I knew it was unlikely. Similarly, if someone wanted to get together with me and I knew it wasn't going to happen (or I didn't want it to happen), I might say, "Sure, let's do that sometime." Or maybe I would say I had a great connection with God during my morning devotions when, in fact, my mind drifted all over the place. I'm talking about gaps as "innocent" as that.

I became deeply committed to making sure my walk matched my talk. I got obsessed with it, in every aspect of my life. That meant if I had a lousy time with God, I had to say so. It meant if I knew I couldn't meet with someone, I had to tell the person that I wasn't going to do it, as disappointing as that was to both of us. It meant if I didn't like food served to me, I had to admit it wasn't to my liking (gently).

It's painful to live this way. Very painful. Recently, Toni and I were in Austin, Texas, for a few days. I was scheduled to speak later that week, but we had a morning off and were going to attend my friend Buck's church. Toni was in charge of Google Maps that morning, and I was behind the wheel. Let's just say my control-freak tendencies and impatience bubbled to the surface one too many times until, out of frustration, I grabbed her phone and said in the most condescending and frustrated tone I could muster, "I'll just read the map myself."

I failed Husbanding 101 that morning, badly. My exam had a big red zero on it. I was so insensitive that Toni broke down in tears, and I pulled over to the side of the road. As we sat there, I tried to make it better in five minutes so we wouldn't be late. You know the kind of "guy move" I'm talking about: *Let's address this as quickly and briefly as possible, so we can get on with things.*

Her frustration with me was so much deeper than any thin attempt I could undertake to make it better. It was just one of those mornings, and she had every right to be angry with me. It's not like it was the first time that ever happened. I was a jerk, and I caused a deep level of heartbreak and disappointment in her (again). This would take a while to work through.

As things got worse, I also knew I had to text my friend to let him know we weren't going to make the services that morning. But the question was what to say. Should I just shoot a quick text that said, "Hey, man, something came up and we can't make it today"? Or should I twist the truth and say, "Sorry, Buck, Toni's not feeling well, so we won't be there"?

I was convicted by two things that morning. First, I had been a terrible friend and husband to Toni. And second, I needed to be honest about what was happening. So I texted my friend Buck and said, "We won't be at church this morning. I was a jerk husband today, and it's just not a good morning for us. I'm so sorry. I'll explain later."

Ugh. Do you know how much it stinks to send a text like that? When I saw Buck and his wife two days later, I owned my failure again, explained the situation, and apologized.

Let me tell you what happens when you are relentlessly committed to making sure your talk matches your walk: you change your walk. Every time I line up my public talk to match my private walk, it makes my private walk better. Words have that kind of power if they're honest. The shame and humiliation of admitting who you really are to people you respect and admire will motivate a big shift in behavior.

People often say, "Well, I have an accountability partner I'm brutally honest with." By that, they usually mean they have an intentional friendship where they talk honestly about their struggles. That's fantastic, and everyone should cultivate those relationships. But your accountability partner isn't with you twenty-four hours a day. Your words and behavior are. Plus, you can spin the story to your advantage when you talk to your accountability partner.

If you simply make your talk match your walk, the gap between who you are and who you want to be becomes smaller almost instantly. It's just too embarrassing to tell the truth, so you make the truth better. Of all the lies we tell, the lies we tell ourselves are the deadliest. One of the best things you can do to overcome your hypocrisy is to humble your talk and accelerate your walk.

If you start becoming ridiculously honest with your self-talk and public talk, does this mean you'll be perfect? Of course not. But it does mean your life will have much more authenticity to it. You'll have the humility to admit your shortcomings, and while that's terrifying at first, it's ultimately liberating. You might be afraid that people will think less of you if you admit your shortcomings. Actually, the opposite is true. People won't think less of you when you're honest. They'll think more of you.

3. Put Yourself First When It Comes to Personal Growth

If you're going to spend twice as much time developing your character as you do developing your competency, it's going to take intentionality. First of all, you need to understand that it is *not* selfish to put yourself first when it comes to personal growth. Which is more egocentric: to compromise again and again until your family no longer respects you and your coworkers distrust you or to take time every day to become a person of deep integrity and honor?

The key words there are *take time every day.* Since nobody is going to give you extra time to become a better person, you need to take it. It means you won't be available to others 24/7. It means you're going to steal away to pray, study, and work on your character. It means you're going to read a book, study the Scriptures, meet with a mentor, take a course, or see a counselor. The time you spend working on your character is an investment in yourself and in the people who matter most to you. It's an investment that pays back in every aspect of your life.

If you think this is unnecessary or that you don't have time for it, just know that Jesus prepared for thirty years before ministering for three. Think about that. His preparation-to-implementation ratio was 10:1. For every year he taught and served and healed, he prepared for ten. And even during those three years, he often disappeared to pray.

Guess what most of us do? We reverse the equation. For every hour of preparation, we pursue activities for ten hours. To be honest, we probably spend an hour preparing for every *hundred* (or even *thousand*) hours of implementation. What if we decided to follow Jesus's example and change our ratio from 1:10 to 10:1? Undoubtedly, doing so would dramatically influence our personal growth and spiritual effectiveness.

With this in mind, set about building a solid spiritual, emotional, and relational foundation for your life. Cancel some appointments. Tell the kids to wait. Pray. Open the Bible. Go for a run. Eat something healthy. Spend time reflecting and journaling. Listen to inspiring music. Meet with a friend who enriches your life.

The only way I know to do these things is to schedule time for them. For me these days, it means I spend the first thirty to sixty minutes of my day reading Scripture, praying, and reflecting. I don't want to make this sound more spiritual than it is. I follow a Bible plan that takes me through three to five passages of Scripture each day. I'm not disciplined enough to make it through the whole Bible in a year if I don't follow a plan. If I'm not careful, my prayer life can be scattered and descend into creating to-do lists or thinking random thoughts that kind of pass as prayers. And my reflections can take me anywhere. But still, the rhythm of this discipline keeps my compass pointed in the right direction.

I also budget time for things like bike rides, hikes, and even yard work. I almost always do these things alone. Sometimes I'll pop in earbuds and listen to a podcast or an audiobook. Sometimes I roll my favorite playlist. And at other times, I'm just silent. It's here that I do not only my best thinking but also some of my best praying and reflecting. The wide-open space of solitude helps me think through the deepest issues I'm facing in life and leadership in a way that an office or home environment never does.

Time with friends to intentionally reflect, work on your issues, and even pray together is time well spent. Those kinds of relationships are rare and need to be cultivated. When you have them, their value becomes immediately apparent.

Times like these will never happen if you don't book them in your calendar. That's why you need to decide how to spend your time before everyone else decides how to spend it for you. Whatever you need to do to ensure you have time to work on your character, do it. Even carving out a few minutes a day to reflect, pray, examine, confess, learn, stretch, plan, and change is a wonderful thing.

Toward an Uncompromised Life

Looking inside and realizing who you've become often causes deep pain, but the payoff is huge. The soul work of character regeneration is far reaching and is at the heart of what Christians often call spiritual maturity. For many in Western culture, spiritual maturity has been defined by how much you know about Scripture, about God, and about the Christian faith. Sadly, the people who claim to be the most mature Christians are often judgmental, divisive, and self-righteous. This isn't maturity at all. In fact, it's just the opposite.

Jesus had a very different end in mind for the spiritually mature. He didn't define maturity by how much you *know.* He defined it by how much you *love.*[6] Working on your character twice as hard as you do on your competency will lead you into the place where God's love regenerates everything about you.

Think about what gets transformed in your life when you commit to the development of your character: Honesty. Love. Kindness. Faithfulness. Trustworthiness. Humility. Compassion. Courage. Faith. Resiliency.

Patience. Perseverance. Self-control. Self-discipline. It's these things that form your character, which in turn ultimately determines your capacity.

Just ask some great athletes who aren't allowed to play anymore.

Just talk to some unemployed executives.

Just ask the politician who had to resign from office.

Just ask the actor no one will work with.

Just ask the preacher with no pulpit.

Competency gets you in the room. Character keeps you in the room. For all of us, it's our character that determines how we'll be remembered. More important, it's our character that God is most interested in. Reverse the compromise that's happening in your life, and you will finally close the gap between who you are and who you want to be. Your interior life will finally begin to sync with your exterior life. Not only will you experience a newfound peace and even deepened humility and self-respect, but you will change your legacy. The people closest to you will become the people most grateful for you.

PART III

DISCONNECTION

5

IS ANYONE OUT THERE?

Why So Many of Us Feel So Alone

I remember getting my first smartphone when BlackBerry was king. My model was the first color screen the company ever released. I was mesmerized. Suddenly, I could be connected anytime, anywhere. Even at dinner. Even on family night. Even on vacation. As you might imagine, my family was not nearly as enthralled with my new phone as I was. Back in the pre-iPhone days, I was the only one with a device in my house, and the only thing I could see was my perspective. I ignored people with great abandon while I scrolled and clicked, and I thought my new technology was the best thing ever.

That all changed when, a few years later, my loved ones all got phones and screens of their own. Suddenly, *I* began to feel ignored. I couldn't believe Toni would text a friend while sitting next to me in the car rather than engage in a riveting conversation with me. Or that she would half answer a question I asked before dinner while she scrolled through her favorite social media.

I was mystified that as I tried to have a meaning-of-life conversation with one of my sons around the kitchen island, he would only occasionally look up and grunt poorly timed affirmations while he smiled at whatever his friends were saying online.

Nothing feels quite as strange as people treating you as poorly as you regularly treat them. It brings out an indignation that only the hypocritical can truly appreciate. How little did I realize that what I began to experiment with back then would soon become the new normal for nearly everyone.

WE'VE NEVER BEEN MORE CONNECTED

It goes without saying that almost anywhere you go, people's eyes are locked on their devices. Couples in restaurants ignore each other while waiting for their salads and blankly, endlessly scroll down. In so many ways, it's a paradox. We've never been more connected as a culture, yet we've never felt more disconnected. Most of us are connected to hundreds, even thousands, of people via social media and other online platforms. As a result, we all now have friends who aren't even really friends; we're just *connected*, whatever that means.

Is there an upside? Sure. I love being able to learn from world-class experts anywhere, anytime. I appreciate being able to text a friend who lives a thousand or ten thousand miles away. I like being able to keep up on everything, including people's vacations, work life, and family moments—even what they're doing on a Thursday at three in the afternoon.

But, like you, it also means that too often I'm more focused on the people I'm not physically with than the people in the room. We've become strangely accustomed to devices in our pockets that buzz, ring, and chirp. The constant buzzing is no respecter of time or occasion. It doesn't care whether it's interrupting lunch, a picnic by the beach, your favorite song, a life-giving conversation on the back porch, or even sex. Our devices have an uncanny ability to interrupt anything significant.

What it means for most of us is that a devious disconnect is underway. You and I are connecting with people, just not the people who are in the room with us. We're having conversations, just not with the people we love most. As a result, we're sacrificing prime time to people we can't hug or touch or see face to face. We might find ourselves paying more attention to someone we knew in college than the people closest to us right now.

We live in a world where you can have five hundred friends and still feel isolated and abandoned. *Solitude* is a gift from God. Isolation is not—it's a tool of the Enemy. As a culture, the more connected we've become, the more isolated we've grown. This is our strange twenty-first-century paradox: we're connected to more people than ever before and we've never felt more alone.

WHO'S TO BLAME?

It's easy to point your finger at technology and decry its evilness. Parents freak out at the addiction to gaming or social media they see in their preteen and teenage kids. Spouses blame their marriage problems on five-inch or sixty-five-inch screens their partners can't pull themselves away from. The problem, after all, must be the technology. Because surely we didn't behave this way when we were kids. Our parents never had problems like this.

Sure, there is emerging evidence that our obsession with tech is not good for us. Former Silicon Valley executives are going on record saying it's not good for our brains, our relationships, or even our ability to focus and do deep work. A growing number of those in the tech industry have begun to speak out against the effect of the very things they created. Increasingly, I share those concerns as well.

But is it really that easy? Just throw our devices under the bus (maybe literally) and everything gets better? Not so fast. Let's think through technology at a more nuanced level. What if, despite its challenges and dangers, technology isn't good or evil but simply reveals and amplifies what's already there?

At some level, isn't saying technology is evil kind of like saying paper is evil? Paper has been used to craft love letters and issue death threats, to write constitutions and to issue declarations of war. Paper has been turned into airplanes by second graders and into fire-starting fuel by arsonists. Is paper evil? You could hardly say it is.

Similarly, couples were breaking up long before they began finding their perfect match online, and families had trouble communicating for generations before videogames captured the minds and thumbs of preteen boys.

Technology does a good job of revealing what's already inside you. If you're narcissistic by nature, social media gives you a new platform to express your self-centeredness. If you lean toward workaholism, you'll always have access to your office as you carry your devices with you everywhere. If you're inclined to look outside your marriage or current relationship for intimacy, it's easier than ever before and takes far less courage than it used to. Technology didn't *create* these issues. It just reveals them and amplifies them. What we're facing is not a technology problem but a human problem.

Conversely, technology can also reveal and amplify magnificent things. It gives us the means to help others and draw attention to important causes. It allows us to crowdsource funding to assist the needy or people who innovate. It gives us the ability to communicate with friends and family members when we're away from one another. It can keep us informed about vital issues around the world. And it can allow people with little access to information or education to gain an edge. In essence, technology is like money:

it makes a terrible master but a wonderful servant. Technology can be used for tremendous good, and it can bring out the worst inclinations in us all.

Not a New Problem

Let's wind the clock back a little further. Before I got my first smartphone, I *already* had a propensity to relationally disconnect from people around me. My new device simply gave me a more convenient way to do that. It didn't create selfish disconnection; it just revealed what was already there.

My challenge goes back to childhood. I was born on a farm, and a few years later my family moved into a brand-new late-sixties three-bedroom bungalow in town. I loved that house. And I loved the friends I made as I started school, played baseball, climbed dirt piles, and rode bikes. But this much-enjoyed and well-connected season of life didn't last.

I remember the day the for-sale sign went up in our yard. My friend Jack and I were talking about how bad it would be to move. He was a great friend, and I wouldn't get to see him anymore. Everything in my eight-year-old body wanted to rip that sign right out of the lawn and throw it away. But I was too timid, scared, and obedient to even try.

A few months later, we moved into a new house in a different city. I started to make friends, and my new best friend lived just a few doors down. Robbie and I became fast buddies, spending as much time together as we could. Eighteen months after we moved there, my dad had a new opportunity, this one three hundred miles away. Another home sale and a five-hour drive later, we arrived in our new home. Sort of. The house wasn't ready, and I finished fourth grade in a school I knew I wasn't going to attend again.

We moved yet another time, just a few miles down the road into a new school district. This meant I started fifth grade with a whole new crew of kids. It was my third school in three years. I distinctly remember making a decision one day in fifth grade: I wouldn't make new friends anymore. It was too painful. I could make it on my own.

Ironically, I spent the next three years in that school, completing my elementary years there. Although we changed houses a few more times, we never left the school district, and I sailed through high school with many of the same kids. Still, I felt like I never fully fit in. I was on the periphery of the cool-kids circle in high school, but I didn't feel like I really belonged. I felt like a permanent outsider. My tendency to keep people at a distance was set. And I've been battling that all my life.

I'm not angry with my parents or with God for any of that. I believe God uses all things and redeems all things, including dumb decisions by ten-year-olds to never make friends anymore. All I'm saying is that the tendency to disconnect is deeply embedded in me.

I'm also obsessed with technology enough to be the guy who's up at 3:00 a.m. ordering the latest devices on release day. My electronic graveyard is vast. My tech usage reveals my bias toward disconnecting in person. And if I'm not careful, that's where I'll end up again and again.

My childhood experience was hardly uncommon. We all knew kids whose families were deeply disconnected. They had the dad who disappeared into the garage with a beer to work on his '68 Camaro, a project that never seemed to get done. Or the mom who was never off the phone and went shopping at the mall all day by herself. Or the sister who locked the door to her room and never came out. Or the older brother who always hung out at his friends' houses and rarely at his own.

Distance between humans is an age-old problem. Long before there was a device in every pocket, front-porch living had given way to backyard isolation. Most people close the garage door after work and close off their lives. In many neighborhoods, next-door neighbors don't know each other—and don't even know each other's names.

A great irony of our age is that the typical regulation to use a high-occupancy vehicle (HOV) lane on a major highway in North America is a car carrying *two* people. Think about it: *high* occupancy is you plus one other person. And guess what? Most of the time you can't use that lane because you don't qualify. Neither does most of the rest of humanity. Thousands of people may be in close proximity to us or simply a finger tap away, but somehow we all feel a little lonelier. The problem is deeper than digital.

Ever Watch *Little House on the Prairie*?

As you'll see later in this book, I'm a fan of change. Without it, we stagnate or even die. And while the results of change are always mixed, change has brought much good into the world. But change creates casualties as well.

My grandfather was born in 1898 and died in 1977. The changes he saw in his lifetime must have been overwhelming at times. He was born into a horse-and-buggy world but lived to see a planet full of cars, airplanes, and space travel, not to mention the arrival of then-fledgling companies like Apple and Microsoft.

Perhaps more remarkable than the technological revolution happening before our eyes is the speed at which it's happening. One hundred years ago, when my grandfather was a young man, people were lucky if they read the equivalent of fifty books of information in a *lifetime*.[1] Think about that for a minute. Typical folks read sparingly, often not because they lacked desire or even ability but because they lacked access to information.

Imagine the pace of life in 1898. Your circle of friends was small and local, most likely people who lived nearby. You might travel a few dozen miles on a day trip to a neighboring village to trade or shop or visit a relative, but that was rare and special. You went to bed shortly after the sun set and woke when it rose. You saw the same people day in and day out in the market, on the street, or at church. And when you weren't working long hours, you engaged in conversation, played games, listened to music, knitted, sewed, read, or took up a hobby.

If you want a snapshot of the pace and tone of life more than a century ago, try watching the two-hour pilot episode of *Little House on the Prairie*. I don't watch much TV, but recently as I was scrolling through options, I spotted *Little House* and, for some reason I still don't understand, I impulsively bought the entire series. As I watched that first episode, I was struck by several things, primarily the pace. The show is set in the 1870s and '80s, just a few decades before my grandfather's birth, and the pace is slow . . . as in molasses-and-peanut-butter-had-a-baby slow. It's so slow there's almost no plot. The family is homesteading in Minnesota, but beyond that, the plot amounts to this: "I cut some wood today. Is there chicken stew for supper? Let's all sit around while we mend socks."

The cinematography, music, and unfolding story lines also struck me. Typical of the way shows were shot in the 1970s, the music is slow, the scenes are slow, and the dialogue is, well, very slow. The camera lingers on characters for a long time, with no reaction shots or jump-cut edits. The drama, such as it is, unfolds at a leisurely pace. And the computer graphics and stunts? Well . . . the difference between that show and the latest superhero movie is staggering—and, I think, refreshing.

If *Little House on the Prairie* teaches us anything, it's how much life has changed over the decades—not only since the late 1800s but also since the show was filmed in the 1970s and 1980s. There is so much unhurried space in *Little House,* so much room for relationships, so much easy conversation, so much time to tend the garden. All of that, frankly, eludes most of us these days. Perhaps most of all, this television program shows us how much we've lost connection to other people.

THE DEATHS OF TWO GOOD FRIENDS

All of this leads us to important questions: What are the rapid change of pace and instant connectedness to millions of people actually *doing* to us? What's happening to our souls, to intimacy, to *us*?

At a macro level, we're dealing with issues we likely won't fully diagnose, let alone solve, for decades. History books will present a more incisive perspective on our times than we can ascertain now. In essence, we are technology's parent—we invented all this—but we're also its child. We've created things we don't fully understand and are not sure how to relate to. And it's changing us. I suspect some of this is exposing the root of our disconnection. In my lifetime, I've noticed the decline—perhaps the near death—of two vital things I see sliding further into the abyss with each passing year. Their demise may be part of the reason people feel so distant from others.

1. The Demise of Genuine Conversation

Great conversation is a beautiful art. It involves the exchange of ideas between two or more people who care enough about one another to listen as well as speak. Sadly, conversations seem to be devolving into an exchange of monologues among people who don't seem terribly interested in one another. People today appear to be talking *at* one another more than they're talking *with* one another. Next time you're in a conversation with someone, wait to see how often you get asked a question. It might be as simple as "How are you doing, really?" or "That's fascinating—can you tell me more?" Questions are the turning points for great conversation and intriguing connections among people.

A number of years ago, I started to notice that people were asking significantly fewer questions in conversation than I had observed before.

Often, people just blurt out a string of mini-monologues that have nothing to do with the individuals they are talking to. It's a sign of genuine disinterest in the listeners' experiences and stories. Look for this pattern of monologue posing as dialogue and you'll start to see it everywhere: at parties, in casual conversations, at dinner with friends, with your family. People talk right past one another, apparently completely disinterested in or oblivious to the individuals with whom they're speaking. I don't remember conversation being this deadening or disheartening a decade or two ago. Yet something within our nature remembers that stimulating conversation is supposed to be mutual.

So where does this decline come from? My theory is that we've grown used to posting status updates, telling the world what's on our mind. Social media has made us all mini-broadcasters. As "social" as social media is, it's still largely a monologue. Most people tell rather than ask. And if you jump into the fray with a comment, it's usually only to air your point, idea, or current state of mind.

I think we've now taken what we do on social media and transported it to live human interactions. We have started assuming other people are infinitely interested in our lives the way they appear to be online. In our self-absorbed minds, we're all Hollywood figures whose lives are endlessly interesting to others, or at least we're too insecure to admit otherwise. Conversation has become a press conference with whomever happens to be listening.

Sadly, it's soul deadening not only to our hearers but also to you and me as speakers. If you converse only in monologues, you will eventually feel deep loss. You'll never discover the joy of truly engaging another human. You'll miss out on other ideas, opposing points of view, and fascinating perspectives you've never considered. You'll never discover how the people you supposedly care about are doing. You'll miss out on the love and delight of one another.

2. The Death of Confession

Beyond the death of genuine conversation, there's an even deeper loss happening: confession seems to be disappearing. Depending on your background, you might think of confession as something that happens in a boxlike booth where you divulge all your sins to a priest. Others of us aren't acquainted with that type of practice, so we tend to shut up about our sins publicly and not really do much about them privately . . . until we commit the offense again. Neither is really confession at its finest. The type of confession I'm talking about has a much broader and far deeper meaning. While the relationship between confession and feeling disconnected may seem tenuous, hang with me for a bit. The two are much more connected than you might think.

Confession is the part of prayer and life where we come before God and one another to admit all that we aren't: our shortcomings, our intentional sins, and myriad unintentional sins. When we confess our brokenness, we admit that we are not all we pretend to be, hope to be, or could be. We own up to the fact that we are a mess.

Confession is hard for many reasons in the best of circumstances. But culturally, we tend to resist the very idea that it's necessary. We have developed a collective allergy to the application of the word *sin* to our lives. After all, nobody really makes mistakes anymore. There's always a scapegoat. It might have been your tough upbringing or your absent father or your overbearing mother or your boss who didn't like you. It might have been your first spouse and, more recently, your second who's causing all the angst in your life. It's definitely not you.

We avoid confession because it requires us to look in the mirror. It demands revealing the real you that you don't want anyone to see. This is the you God would love for you to bring to him, but you (and I) steadfastly refuse to surrender. The shift away from confession leaves most of us in a precarious state, particularly younger adults, teens, and kids who were raised in a society that ignores sin. Furthermore, for a few generations now, parents have embraced a philosophy that compliments and praises a child for pretty much everything that child does, with seeming disregard to a child's actual performance, ability, or effort.

As Dr. Tim Elmore has chronicled, narcissism is on the rise in young adults and kids: "In the 1950s, when teens were asked if they were a 'very important person,' less than ten percent said they were. Fifty years later, more than 80 percent said they were." Elmore says our approach to parenting is producing a generation of kids who suffer from "high arrogance, low self-esteem."[2] Healthy self-esteem is developed when praise is linked to actual accomplishment and effort, Elmore says. This is a much healthier understanding of self because it acknowledges the vital role that failure, struggle, and confession play in life.

Here's what I've realized in my life: confession and progress are inexorably linked. You won't address what you don't confess. If you think about this more deeply, it's the things that you refuse to confess that grate on the relationships that matter to you. Your unwillingness to address your critical words drives a wedge down the center of your marriage. Your self-absorption builds a wall between you and your kids, not to mention your friends. Jealousy and envy make it impossible to celebrate the accomplishments of anyone else, and your friendships stay shallow or dissolve as a result.

It's like our culture has created the perfect storm for disconnection. We all carry the illusion that we're deeply connected through our devices, yet at the same time our (always justified) obsession with our own stories is leading us to ignore others and to refuse to confess our root problems. It's never us after all, is it?

It's no wonder we feel so disconnected.

Our lack of confession disconnects us from God, from one another, and even from ourselves. So what do we do? Do we just shut off all our devices, go live on a mountain, and commune with nature? Hardly. But you might try some of what follows next.

DITCHING YOUR PHONE WON'T HELP

Why You Need to Solve the Human Problem

Y ou might think that the cure for disconnection is just to put down your phone. And, sure, that will help. I've attempted periods of technological abstinence and had moderate success. It's possible to live without technology for a few days or longer. You can learn to live without the constant need to see what's happening outside your immediate square footage.

But ditching technology is not the real solution to our problems. It's like living in the early twentieth century and thinking you'll always keep your horse and carriage. As people of that generation learned, the internal combustion engine wasn't going away anytime soon. Neither are the internet and the electronic devices in our day. The challenge is not to *resist* change but to learn how to *thrive* in the midst of it. After all, disconnection is a human problem. Technology just makes it worse.

For that reason, let's pick up where we left off in the previous chapter, with confession as a conduit to connection. The challenge is to stop blaming others and to take responsibility for your own sins. Blame is insidious, as it will keep showing up in your mind to convince you that nothing is your fault.

As I've reflected on this over the years, I've come to see critical differences between four key concepts: excuses, reasons, explanations, and justifications. *Excuses* find their genesis in the reasons things didn't go the way you hoped. Yes, your parents got a divorce when you were six years old. Sure, your coach never put you in the games when you deserved to play. No, it's not fair that other kids got their education paid for while you couldn't attend the college of your choice. But here's the question you need to answer: When are your past circumstances going to stop defining your present and future? At a certain point, your circumstances have to stop functioning as excuses.

Reasons function in a similar way in the present tense. Yes, there are reasons your marriage is bad. There are reasons your self-esteem is low. There are reasons you struggle at work. I get that. Yet as real as those reasons are, most of the time in our thought life and prayer life, we focus on the things we *can't* control. We demand our spouse to change, our kids to treat us better, or our boss to behave fairly. But when are you going to stop focusing on what you can't control and instead start focusing on what you *can* control? What if for one month you prayed only about things within your control? Well, to begin with, I think you would stop making excuses.

So then, you ask, what do I do? Do I just ignore my past? Pretend the divorce never happened? Pretend my heart has never been broken? Deny the bad things that happened along the way? Absolutely not. But instead of using those experiences as *excuses,* try to view those pivotal moments in your life as *explanations* that can lead to transformation. The language of explanation is different from the language of excuse. Explanation carries with it a tone of inquiry.

Thomas Edison lived through thousands of unsuccessful attempts to produce a better light bulb, yet he never considered those failed attempts as justifications for abandoning the project; each became one more explanation that led to his world-changing breakthrough. Edison famously said, "I have not failed 10,000 times. I have not failed once. I have succeeded in proving that those 10,000 ways will not work. When I have eliminated the ways that will not work, I will find the way that will work."[1] Explanations are the fuel of the curious, the brave, and the driven. When you search for an explanation as to why you have a hard time trusting or opening your heart to people, you can make progress. You're using the past as a stepping-stone into the future, not as a barricade against it.

When you stop using your past as a justification, you'll also begin to realize that maybe, just maybe, you have problems for which you are responsible. True, you didn't cause your parents' divorce, but you've chosen to hang on to the hurt long past its expiration date. You've refused to look inside, to forgive, to ask God to help you heal. When you start to confess your failures, your refusal to make excuses helps you make progress. You're confessing your role, and you're changing because of it.

Healthy people treat reasons as *explanations,* not justifications. Justifications lead to stagnation and, eventually, either to complete denial ("I'm responsible for nothing") or to self-pity ("Woe is me; I'm stuck here forever"). Self-pity chisels into stone what discouragement whispers.

Thousands of people face the same set of circumstances every day. The biggest difference between those who make progress and those who make excuses is how they treat the reasons for the circumstances. You get to pick: you can see a reason as a justification that leads to stagnation or as an explanation that can lead to transformation. Start confessing your role. Start shedding the past. Start owning your shortcomings. Because you can make excuses or you can make progress, but you can't make both.

FOSTER THE ART OF CONVERSATION

Once you begin confessing your sins, you'll begin to see yourself as the problem and God's transformation of you as the solution in your relationships. It will also reduce your self-absorption and self-justification. You will begin to develop a heart for others, which should transform your conversations and begin to foster better relationships. Life-giving conversation is a back-and-forth exchange in which people take an active interest in one another. Think of it as a Ping-Pong match. If you hold the ball too long, you're not really playing.

What happens if the conversation is not mutual, if you keep gently volleying questions and get nothing in return but long-winded answers? Be the adult in that case and continue to ask questions. A remotely healthy person will pick up on the change in dynamic over time and begin to foster mutuality in the dialogue. An unhealthy or self-absorbed person won't.

So what about the self-absorbed conversationalist? Well, you can choose your friends, but you can't really choose your family or your coworkers. You'll likely always have a few strained relationships in your life. However, even frustrating conversations can be exercises in both humility and spiritual growth. When you take an interest in others more than in yourself, it's a very small form of dying to yourself, something very close to the heart of Christ. When you give your life away, something great rises.

For me, the sense that a conversation is going nowhere always carries with it an underpinning of judgment and even arrogance on my part. I just assume I'm better, smarter, or wiser or that I have greater emotional intelligence than others. Which, of course, should drive me right back to my knees in confession. After all, we're encouraged to think of others as better than ourselves. That's a cornerstone habit of the humble.[2]

In addition to what I've already outlined, several other things will happen when you elevate the level of conversation with the people around you. First, you'll genuinely learn about how others are, which will foster a meaningful connection with them. Second, people are starved for real conversation. You'll discover that your relationships become far more life giving. Third, you'll soon move beyond the "How are you?" kind of conversation and start talking about deeper things. You'll move beyond people and events and start to have life-giving conversations about ideas, possibilities, truth, dreams, hopes, and ambitions. Your level of thinking will elevate. Finally, you may even find yourself being sought after as a friend, confidant, or mentor. The skill of meaningful conversation is so rare these days that when people find it, it's like they've discovered a treasure, which, of course, they have.

DISCONNECT TO GET CONNECTED

Another way to connect with other people is to disconnect from technology from time to time. Remember what I said previously: I'm a techie, and I love my gadgets. But a few years ago, I became a reluctant convert to the discipline of disconnecting. The insidiousness of having work with me wherever I walk, sit, or run deeply affects my soul and relationships. Even if I'm not working, I know I could be. And the temptation to work creates a constant urgency and obsession that's hard to resist.

Flash back to my BlackBerry days. I love my family's response to my first smartphone obsession: they went all out to preserve their relationships with me. While I was connecting with lots of people, I wasn't connecting with the most important people—my family. They fought for my heart. I wish I had seen earlier what was happening, but I'm so glad *they* saw it.

Over the last few years, I've made drastic changes in how we relate as a family, recognizing how technology is increasingly and dramatically affecting our personal lives. I want to make sure that any electronic device I use will enrich my life—especially my family life—and not erode it. So let me share some strategies I've learned to make sure technology doesn't own me like it used to:

- My family members and I shut off everything (except background music) at dinner. No phones and no TV—just conversation and food. We try to eat at home together as a family five or six times a week. That's a sit-down-and-chat kind of mealtime. We recently remodeled our kitchen to make it even easier to cook together and eat together. Rather than cooking *for* our guests all the time, we've recrafted the space so it's easy to work on meals together—a shared communal experience. In an era of constant distraction and busyness, food created in a home setting can provide an almost sacramental connection.

- I no longer use my phone in the car when I have someone with me. I (wince) used to catch up on phone calls when my wife or kids were with me. Not anymore. Being together in the car is a great chance to talk about anything and everything. I've never owned a vehicle with a video system for the same reason. Drive time can and should be quality time.

- We play board games—good old-fashioned board games like Monopoly, Clue, or Scrabble. No checking texts, emails, or Facebook during family game time.

- We look for activities to do together, whether that's hiking, biking, or boating. It gets us out of our typical routine and encourages conversation.

- We invite family and friends into our home—and linger. Unhurried time with people close to us, sharing stories and experiences, enriches our lives and fosters connection.

- We go on vacations together. It's amazing to me how we instinctively put our phones and other devices away when we're on holiday. We might check the next day's weather forecast or search the internet for activities to do, but mostly the devices are set aside. Every year we spend a week at a place where our phones don't even work and there are no TVs. My kids call it their favorite place on earth.

- I put my phone on "do not disturb" mode all day long. This means I don't hear a *ding* or feel a vibration, so my conversations, thoughts, and work are not interrupted. The reality is I can check to see if I've missed anything urgent when I have a free moment. If the house is really on fire, I'm sure someone will track me down and let me know it's burning.

- I no longer sleep with any electronics in my bedroom. I used to charge my phones on my nightstand, but several years ago I moved them to my home office. The result has been much better sleep.

WHAT'S YOUR HURRY?

You might be like me in this way: I love to run hard, push the limits, and squeeze the most out of every day. And our connected world has made that possible in a way that previous generations couldn't have imagined. We've never had more access to information or opportunity. This often amps up the pressure we feel to do more, be more, and accomplish more. We have amazing opportunities at our fingertips, but this brings concerns. We hear a lot about our accelerated pace of life and for good reason. The speed at which we travel is exciting but also problematic. I have discovered that a hurried life leads to an unexamined and disconnected life. Hurry kills intimacy with God, with family, and with friends.

Slowing down your pace is the only way you can pause long enough to confess the mess you are in and the mess you've created. It's the only way you can engage the people around you. It's the only way you can be truly present with your family.

Love has a speed. And it's slower than I am. There's a good chance it's slower than you are. Love pauses. Love lingers. Love offers full focus and gives far more than it takes. When I run too fast, I outrun love, and the people I love pay a price.

Do I still run hard? Sure I do. But I've also built margin into my life, which I never had before I burned out. My day starts with thirty to sixty minutes of time to pray and read Scripture, no matter where I am. I've cut out many of the meetings that used to occupy much of my workday. I've also integrated more sleep and rest into my calendar. The point is, the world may not be slowing down anytime soon, but that doesn't mean you can't. You really can.

Here's something else I have observed: the leaders I admire most and who have accomplished the most tend to be people who never seem in a rush, who have all the time in the world. There's something to that. John Ortberg became a close friend of theologian and author Dallas Willard, one of the spiritual giants of his generation. In the early days of their friendship, John was caught up in the hustle and hubbub of a growing ministry, as well as the endless soccer games and school events that characterize family life.

One day John asked Dallas what he should to do to become more spiritually healthy.

After a long pause, Dallas replied, "You must ruthlessly eliminate hurry from your life."

John wrote down that advice and waited for more, perhaps something more profound. He finally said, "What else is there?"

Another long pause.

"There is nothing else," Dallas said. "You must ruthlessly eliminate hurry from your life."[3]

Of course, Dallas and John are right. Hurry kills so many things, including intimacy. So what would it take for you to really slow down? What would it take for you to stop rushing? What would it take for you to just put down the phone, look into the eyes of the people you care about, and connect? What would it take for you to cross some activities off your to-do list and add people instead? What would it take for you to slow down long enough to hear the sound of your breath as you pray and reflect, to rest in the quiet that has eluded you for so long?

In the process of connecting with others, you might finally connect with God. In addition, something more unfamiliar might happen. You might even connect with yourself.

PART IV

IRRELEVANCE

CHANGE NEVER ASKS PERMISSION

The Silent Creep of Irrelevance

When Toni and I got married, we were students in our midtwenties. We had no money. We took any and all furniture anyone gave us. We accepted an ugly avocado-green couch my friend Alyson was tossing out. For our dining room, we adopted dilapidated seventy-year-old church chairs that I glued back together and painted. We knew none of it would get us any interior design awards, but cheap or free items were what our budget could accommodate. Free beat chic every time.

As we moved into our thirties and then our forties, all those hand-me-downs eventually left our place either for someone else's home or for the dump, where by that point they pretty much belonged. Over the years, as money became available, we replaced them piece by piece with stuff we actually liked. Sure, we always looked for sales, but some of the stuff that we bought on our own *wasn't* cheap. When you sink a few thousand dollars into a well-made living room or bedroom set, you value it differently than the purple chair you found in your uncle's garage. And as a result, you tend to hang on to it.

There are a couple of reasons for this. First, *you* chose the item. Unlike the desperate grab for freebies and discounts from random relatives, friends, strangers, and thrift shops in your younger years, you selected it intentionally. You saved for it. So you're not as eager to drag it to the curb or sell it at a garage sale for fifteen dollars. Second, because an item is new and likely better made than your starter stuff, it tends to not wear out. And if it's perfectly good and still works, why would you get rid of it?

This explains exactly how a trend happens that, for years, I never really understood.

When I started ministry in our little churches as a thirty-year-old, one of the perplexing theological questions I had was this: Why do all the elderly people I visit have furniture and decor that's twenty to thirty years out of date? (Profound question, I know, but I'm deep like that.) I went on a lot of home visits in those early days, and each time I walked through the door I got immersed in the sixties and seventies in a way I hadn't been since I was a kid. There were acres of shag carpet (before it was cool again). There were near museums of teak furniture (before it was cool again). There was an abundance of olive-green and brown appliances (which have never been cool again). Even when it came to personal wardrobe choices, the formal wear of most elderly parishioners was a throwback to loud, wide ties and polyester lapels in an era of thin wool suits. And if the wardrobe happened to be updated a bit, it was usually with the inclusion of a fanny pack from 1985. I felt like I was stepping into a time machine. It always left me wondering if these folks realized time and culture had moved on.

Of course, once I hit my forties and had purchased my own (usually new) things, my perspective changed. I, too, found it harder to get rid of things. I realized *that's* why people stop updating their decor. And, after all, life is more than just furnishings and wardrobe, so why spend the time and money to replace it or update it? There was, by this time, a deep-sunk cost bias, even if what we now owned was growing out of date by the year.

But there's a bigger principle at work. Furniture is one thing. Your life is another. Irrelevance costs you more—far more—when it permeates what you do, how you communicate, and whom you influence.

THE EROSION OF INFLUENCE

Irrelevance happens when the language, methods, or styles you use no longer connect to the culture and people around you. Essentially, you end up speaking a language people no longer understand or appreciate. Irrelevant people eventually lose the ability to communicate meaningfully with the people they care about and to contribute to the causes they're passionate about. Sometimes it leaves them frustrated and confused as to why no one gets them anymore. In other cases, irrelevance leaves them surprisingly unaware that their influence is eroded or just plain gone.

Irrelevance has a sting to it that catches many people off guard. The once-sharp leader is out of work at fifty and almost unemployable. The filmmaker everybody watched a decade ago shows his reels to an audience that grows smaller and older with every passing year. The entrepreneur who had several thriving businesses in his thirties now peddles ideas that just get blank stares—or, worse, looks of pity. The dad who coached Little League and whom kids adored now just sits at home anesthetized by the TV.

Irrelevance can be cruel as it silently squanders your influence. Most of us spend considerable energy and effort in our younger years trying to influence the people we care about and advance the causes that matter to us. Irrelevance sabotages that influence. Without ever telling you why, people quietly dismiss you as someone who doesn't quite get it. They write you off as quaint, outdated, and even insignificant.

THE FASTEST PATH TO IRRELEVANCE

Rick Warren said it well: "When the speed of change around an organization is faster than the speed of change inside the organization, the organization becomes irrelevant."[1] That's also true for people. The gap between how quickly *you* change and how quickly *things* change is called irrelevance. The bigger the gap, the more irrelevant you become.

Let me ask you a difficult question: What's changing faster, you or the culture? Assuming you're being honest with yourself, I believe I know your answer. Consequently, the fastest path to irrelevance is this: stop changing. I'm *not* talking about soul-level change here. Change your value system often, and it won't be long before you've sold your soul, ending up in the trouble we talked about earlier in this book. The goal is not to chase culture, morphing into a different person every season. No, the goal is to understand the culture well enough that you are able to speak into it. And that, of course, requires change and adaptation.

THE BIG FREEZE

So how do once-relevant people become *ir*relevant? We already understand how furniture and decor can get outdated. Understanding the rest isn't much of a leap. We'll discuss career and relational irrelevance in a moment, but let's look at something that shows us how our musical tastes and preferences form. Researchers see an almost universal trend when it comes to the music we listen to as we move through our adult years. Experts think that people's fondness for certain types of music is forged between ages sixteen and twenty-four.[2] I've even heard some people argue that your musical tastes crystalize at twenty-three and follow you the rest of your life. That might explain the fifty-year-old guy still sporting a mullet and rocking out to Metallica or the seventy-five-year-old Deadhead who looks like a much grayer and wrinkled version of himself at twenty-four, when the Grateful Dead first emerged. Some people never evolve past their younger incarnations.

Maybe that's not you. Possibly you've morphed a bit, but take a look at your musical tastes more closely. While your tastes have likely evolved a bit over time, they probably aren't so different from what they were when you were younger. If you loved U2 growing up, you might like Coldplay now,[3] or if you loved Blink 182 in college, you might like Imagine Dragons a little better than, say, Justin Bieber or Bruno Mars. Conversely, someone who owned every Madonna or Backstreet Boys CD in college may lean more toward Bieber or any Top 40 artist these days. The groove that fires the pleasure center in your brain doesn't change much with age. That's the very factor that, as you age, makes you listen to current music and ask yourself how anyone could even call it music.

So what's the point? Unchecked, most of us live in the decade where a lot of our tastes, knowledge, and experiences were shaped. We pick an era we love and, for the most part, stay frozen there. The past has a nostalgia that the future never does. We're more comfortable living with what we know and like than living in what we don't know.

In the same way, you might know an abundance of movie references from when you were dating but be unable to name a single nominee for best picture from last year. Or you can name every player on your favorite baseball team from your teenage years but wouldn't know an all-star pitcher from today's New York Yankees if he passed you on the street. This principle applies to technology as well. You're tired of the constant app updates and new operating systems, so you hang on to your devices as long as you can because, well, you know them.

Of course, if you're twenty-five, you're wondering what on earth I'm talking about. Everything to you is current, easy, and accessible. In fact, change within the culture is almost invisible to you because it's natural and effortless. You smile at your grandma who doesn't quite get social media and puts an article before everything (The Instagram), but your fifty-one-year-old mom just irritates you with her failure to realize that simply phoning people out of the blue isn't that awesome anymore.

Think about it for a minute: What year or decade did you freeze in (or *will* you freeze in if you're younger)? You've seen the big freeze in organizations and company culture too. It's almost like everyone or everything has a year attached to it. You've gone into businesses, offices, stores, restaurants, and schools and thought, *Man, this place looks like 1998, or maybe 1978.* Sometimes a building will even retain the smell of a certain year. If you're not careful, you're going to start to smell like the year you stopped changing.

I had that experience when my oldest son went to high school. He graduated twenty-five years after I did in a town thirty miles away from mine. I graduated from high school in the mideighties. When I walked the halls of his high school, I felt like I had been transported back in time. My son's school was identical to my old one: same desks, same labs, same lockers, same paint scheme. Nothing had changed in twenty-five years. It was shocking to me that so little had been updated since I was in high school a full generation earlier. And it was a little eerie.

Guess what they did to his school the year after he graduated? They tore it down.

Culture Never Asks Permission to Change

Why is irrelevance a natural drift in almost all our lives? Here's the problem: Culture never asks permission to change. It just changes. Nobody has ever knocked on your door and said, "Hey, we're changing car designs and adding a ton of autonomous features, so you'd better be good with self-driving vehicles. Is that okay with you?" Nor will anyone say, "Hey, a bunch of us decided it was rude to not set your phone on silent in public. We secretly changed the rule at midnight, and now everyone who keeps his or her phone ringer on in public will be quietly but firmly shamed. Sound good to you?"

Similarly, fashion never asks permission to change. It's just that one day your favorite jeans have a waistline that's too high or too low, and no one bothered to tell you about it. Your tie is narrower or wider than everyone else's at the wedding. You never got the memo. (Because nobody sends memos anymore anyway.) Slang changes too. If you're still telling people to take a chill pill because you're chillaxing, well, I'm just so sorry. There was a time when it was rad to be as fly as you are, but that time is no more.

Industries transition. Technology evolves. Markets adjust. The economy morphs. Values shift from generation to generation. Even what we call people groups changes, and a phrase that was perfectly acceptable thirty years ago now makes you sound like a bigot when you use it to describe someone's ethnicity today.

If you think about all the change in your lifetime—changes in technology, society, design, fashion, linguistics, music, and culture—it's staggering. And no one had the courtesy to ask you if it was okay. Which is exactly how irrelevance happens. Before you know it, you're the person on the team who gets mocked by the newbies at the watercooler. You've seen a few people roll their eyes when they thought you weren't looking.

Or you're told you just don't have the skill set for the job, and you wonder why the things that worked a decade ago aren't good enough anymore. You sense that talking to your kids is harder than ever, and you can't quite put your finger on why.

Something has shifted. And you were the last to know.

Welcome to irrelevance. The question is, How do you fight it? The good news is there is a way to beat it.

CRAVING DIFFERENT

How Regular (and Radical) Change Keeps You in the Game

Just in case this section of the book feels a little judgmental, please know I'm working hard to keep up too. I have been the victim of a teenage eye roll more than a few times as I tried to do a clean OS install, assemble a new grill, or follow the instruction manual for something new we bought. The inevitable opening phrase was "Here, Dad," said with a tone of exasperation, accompanied by said eye roll, a deep sigh, and the swing of an arm down to grab the manual/tool/device out of my hand so my boys could perform the task ten times faster than I could. In their teenage glory, they would look at me like I'd had my brain removed long before they were born. Both of my sons are in their twenties now, and there's much more grace and even partnership these days. But clearly, *they* are leading *me*. That was established long ago.

So in light of the fact that the next generation will almost always be better/faster/stronger, how do you fight irrelevance? Plain and simple, you keep changing, learning, and evolving. Change staves off irrelevance. I know this sounds simple, but it's not, which is why so many people struggle with change. The older you get, the harder it is to change. If you're young and your native language is current culture, you may be able to navigate the culture in all its nuances without much thought today. But your twenties give way to your thirties, then your forties and beyond. The culture keeps changing. The question becomes, Do you?

The barrier to change, of course, is that anything that deviates from your default—your normal—will feel unfamiliar, challenging, and sometimes even threatening. And every decade, the gap grows between where culture has gone and what you're hardwired to view as "normal." It's not that hard to feel like a stranger in the world you live in. Consequently, change is the only thing that bridges the gap between who you are and who you need to be. Change keeps your job skills fresh and your language up to date. It keeps you connected to your kids and, eventually, grandkids.

"Well," comes the pushback, "what about timeless values and things that never change?" That's a great question. Theologically, God never changes, and for sure, God's values are timeless. But your willingness to change gives you the ability to communicate timeless truths in a way that has meaning to those who come after you. If you want to influence the next generation (or the current one), change is your friend. If you stubbornly cling to outdated methods, soon you'll find yourself selling Kodak film after photography has gone digital or hawking DVDs after movies have gone online. If you're not careful, you'll be the last one to figure out why your approach and skills are not resonating.

All of this probably makes sense to you. But still, many people resist change. So now for the deeper question: Exactly why *is* change so hard for so many?

HERE'S WHY PEOPLE DON'T CHANGE

Change is difficult because you and I are hardwired to resist it. To test that, play along with this scenario: Let's say you know that the all-season tires on your car need to be changed. Yet if you're like most of us, you're inclined to get as much wear and tear out of them as you can. After all, getting four new tires put on a vehicle is a pain.

First, it's expensive. A good set of tires is going to cost you a big chunk of money. Second, it's a hassle. You might need to leave the car at the shop for the day and catch a ride to work with a friend, on the bus, or through Uber. You might need to sit in the waiting room for a few hours, mindlessly scrolling your phone or growing mildly bored watching some daytime show playing on the service lounge TV. No wonder people put off decisions like getting their tires changed.

But let's say that tonight you head out on an errand, your current set of tires still on the vehicle. It's raining, and as you make your way onto the freeway, you notice a sea of red taillights ahead of you. Traffic comes to abrupt halt, and you jam on the brakes to avoid rear-ending the car ahead of you.

Suddenly, your car starts to swerve out of control. You do a complete 360, almost hitting several vehicles around you before you come within inches of the center median. A few seconds later, your car comes to a full stop with other drivers honking and gesturing in no uncertain terms what they think of you.

Once you come to your senses, you look around. Much to your surprise, you realize you haven't hit anything. You're actually *fine*. Miraculously, you escaped doing even minimal damage. Your car—and you—are 100 percent intact. So you slowly take your foot off the brake and head to your destination, unharmed.

Question: What are you going to do first thing tomorrow morning?

Exactly. Get new tires for your vehicle.

Why?

Here's why: You're ready to change because the pain associated with the status quo just became greater than the pain associated with change. That's the moment most of us change. It's why you know you should eat a little less and start exercising, but you don't do it until the doctor tells you that you're headed for diabetes, a heart attack, or both. Suddenly, getting up at six in the morning to run three times a week and passing on the dessert buffet is no longer that difficult. It's why you think your attitude is no big deal until your wife tells you she's so frustrated that she's thinking of leaving you. Finally, you begin to watch the way you talk to her and treat her.

Change is painful. And that's why the vast majority of us resist it. That's why it's just easier to use the sales tactics that worked when you started, even though the market has changed dramatically. That's why it's tempting to just stick with the management philosophy you learned when you graduated, even though your style rubs younger workers the wrong way. That's why you skip workshops and seminars that will teach you new strategies: you figure the old methods are "tried and true."

THE DYNAMICS OF CHANGE

I have spent most of my working life among groups of people who resist change. If you want to talk to people who understand resistance to change, hang out with church leaders for a while. For some reason, North American Christians tend to cling to the past more than they want to leap into the future. The decline of both faith and church attendance during the previous decades has been significant, and the relevance of the church to the culture has suffered as well. In my view, there's a direct correlation between the two phenomena. Yet often Christians believe that since God doesn't change, we don't need to either. I've committed my life to reversing that belief. After all, irrelevance causes us to lose the ability to speak into a culture. There has never been a more important time for the church to have a voice, yet we're at the point of losing ours.

The church may be a prime example of resistance to change, but it's certainly not the only one. In your lifetime, you've seen whole industries change, titans fall, and once-innovative organizations go under. By contrast, a fair number of the largest and fastest-growing companies today didn't even exist thirty years ago. I'm fascinated by why some people and organizations change and others don't.[1] Think about the massive companies and brands that no longer exist or are a shadow of what they used to be: Kodak, Blockbuster, Polaroid, Compaq Computers, Borders, Nokia, Pontiac, and Oldsmobile, just to name a few.

Take Kodak. Case studies show that there was a bitter war inside Kodak between the digital division and the print division. The top executives were fixated on getting people to print their digital photos. The digital division said people didn't care. And yet it's not like Kodak wasn't thinking about digital at all—they just missed its significance. There's more than a little irony in the fact that in 2000 Kodak also launched an early photo upload website, OFoto. But as *Harvard Business Review* notes, instead of making it a place to share pictures, they dedicated the site to getting people to print their pictures.[2] Essentially, they leveraged new technology to prop up an old model, a strategy that ultimately helped do them in.

In many ways, that's what churches and companies are doing today. We're using new technology to prop up an old model. What if leaders started thinking of themselves as a digital organization with a physical presence, instead of a physical organization with a digital presence? After all, everyone they want to reach is already online.

Imagine what might have happened if a decade or so before Kodak folded, Kodak asked itself, "Are we in the *film* business or the *photography* business?" Had they been in the photography business, they might still be the iconic company they used to be. The ultimate irony is that Kodak actually *invented* digital photography; they came out with the first digital camera. You would expect a brand synonymous with photography that invented the digital camera to thrive. Instead, it went bankrupt in 2012.

Ultimately, you know who killed Kodak? It wasn't another digital photography company. It was Instagram. When the game changes that massively, those who refuse to change die.

The newspaper business is another industry rocked to the core by the digital age. One of the most important questions newspaper executives can ask as they watch everything change before their eyes is this: "Are we in the *newspaper* business or the *news* business?"

But what seems obvious to outsiders is rarely that obvious to insiders, which is why you and I struggle badly with change. So that you can see what most of us miss, here are three principles that will help you understand why you resist the change you need to make to stay relevant.

1. You Aren't Opposed to Change, Just Change You Didn't Think Of

Change happens in two ways: it is externally imposed or internally driven. Internally driven change is easier to deal with by far. It's change *you* devised. It's you deciding to write a book, take a course on leadership, change your office hours, or develop new friendships. You're already a fan of it. Will you ever feel resistance to internally driven change? Sure, but not nearly as intensely as the resistance you feel to externally imposed change.[3] When someone else decides you need to be in the office by 8:00 a.m. every day, it's completely different than when *you* decide to arrive at that time.

The challenge with the cultural and social changes that cause you to become irrelevant is that they're all *externally* imposed changes. That kind of change is beyond your control. So you naturally try to do the only thing you can do to exert control over it: ignore it, resist it, or fight it.

2. You Crave What You Already Like

Think about your appetite. You probably don't crave foods you haven't tried, do you? That's because it's virtually *impossible* to crave something you haven't sampled, smelled, or experienced. You don't even have a category for it because your brain struggles to categorize the unknown. As a result, when it comes to your eating habits, you have a built-in bias to eat more of your favorite, go-to food options.

Your work patterns, life habits, decorating tastes, and other preferences all operate the same way. You've cultivated a set of effective strategies, approaches, and routines at work. It's natural to want to repeat and refine what's already proven successful. As a result, new methods often don't look as appealing as the system you've carefully developed and utilized. Your tastes and preferences also behave this way. You're far more likely to put your favorite playlist on repeat than you are to endlessly cycle through music you've never heard before. My wife tells me that when I go shirt shopping, I just buy more of what I already own. And I guess the fact that I have eight checked shirts hanging together in the closet proves she has a point. Because you crave what you already like, your life is liable to keep repeating your established preferences. The brain has a bias toward what it already knows.

3. You Encounter Problems with Success

Usually you become successful because you've embraced change. You found some competitive advantage and retooled it. You started something or were the first to market. That's often how organizations and leaders flourish. But once they achieve a measure of success, a whole other dynamic kicks in.

Surprisingly, success makes you conservative. The more successful you are, the less likely you are to change. When you were starting out, had almost no money, and hadn't accomplished much, what did you have to lose? Pretty much nothing. This is exactly why it was easy to take risks and forge ahead. Since you had little, almost any tiny step forward looked like big progress.

When success comes, you suddenly have something to preserve and conserve, whether that's your net worth, your strategy and tactics, or your practices and habits. There's even your reputation to think about. As a result, you're far less open to change because you don't want to mess with a good thing. You want to stick with the tactics that got you this far.

This is exactly how successful organizations become irrelevant. At one point, department stores were the biggest retailers in the world. Now, most are in steep decline. Rather than adapt, many executives couldn't imagine a world in which consumers wouldn't want to one-stop shop in a physical store. Their highly profitable model worked so well for so long they resisted change . . . until the internet changed everything. Now, Amazon and its ilk are the places for one-stop shopping.

Success often causes those once bold and brazen to become complacent and even fearful. What's true for corporations and organizations is also true for individuals. Things are working so well, why vary the formula? Don't rock the boat. Just stay the course. This is the danger point most successful people and organizations never see coming. That's why the greatest enemy of your future success is always your current success.

WHAT DOES CHANGE LOOK LIKE?

If the antidote to irrelevance is change, what does change look like? How can you tell whether you're in a place to keep innovating, growing, and moving forward? In addition to being aware of why you're biased against change (which we've just seen), here are four insights and strategies to make sure you stay current.

1. Love the Mission More Than the Methods

If you think about your life, most of what you do can be divided into two categories: mission and methods. The mission is big—it's about what you want to accomplish. Methods are smaller and should be subservient to mission. Your methods are what help you achieve your mission.

I am privileged to host a fairly popular leadership podcast. Leaders seem to appreciate it, and the growth curve of the show has been phenomenal. As a result, people often ask me, "So will you always podcast?"

My answer? "No, I don't think so."

Why? Because podcasting is the method, not the mission. My mission is to help people thrive in life and leadership. Podcasting is currently a very effective *method* for helping and teaching people. But I'm sure the day will come when people will take out their earbuds and something else will become even more effective. On that day (or hopefully long before that day comes), I'll ditch podcasting and embrace whatever new method will allow me to help people thrive.

To be successful in life, methods need to serve your mission. This principle shows up everywhere. A few years ago, Toni and I became empty nesters. ("What's that like?" you ask. Honestly, it's amazing. It's like date night every night.) We love our kids. When they lived at home, connecting with them was incredibly easy. We had dinner together almost every night and hung out all the time.

Now that they've moved out of the house, naturally it's more challenging. We've had to change our methods to accomplish our mission. We have flown to the East Coast to visit one son while he studied there. We regularly drive to Toronto to visit our older son. We set aside weekends to be together, and we got a boat to create more shared activities.

Mission and methods often work in harmony, serving hand in hand. But just as often you'll see the two competing. If you're missing the goals you have for your mission, change your methods. The challenge, of course, is that far too many people love their methods more than they love their mission. It would be like Toni and me cooking dinner for four every night and wondering why our kids never show up or like me deciding to podcast long after people stopped listening.

At work and in life, your methods should constantly be changing so you can better accomplish your mission—financially, relationally, spiritually, physically, and in every other facet. Otherwise you become Kodak. If the methods are more important than the mission, you die.

2. Get Radical

We live in an era of radical cultural change, most of which we didn't create and don't control. So we might be tempted to slow down a bit, to think that the change required is not as drastic as others would suggest it is, to try to find some middle ground. I get that. When it comes to staying healthy, for instance, I always try to convince myself I can do the minimum amount of exercise that will allow me to eat the maximum amount of meat. But you and I both know that when it comes to fitness, you reap what you sow. The benefits are commensurate to the effort you put in.

That's the problem with minimal effort. Incremental change brings about incremental results. Furthermore, incrementalism inspires no one. Radical change brings about radical results. If you're in a rapidly changing world, small amounts of personal incremental change are likely not enough.

3. Become a Student of Culture

Regardless of your personal preferences, and even if you don't like today's culture, you can still be a student of it. Honestly, I have to work harder at this with each passing year. My personal musical tastes don't stay as current or mainstream as they did a few decades ago. And I have generally lost interest in movies and even TV compared to when I was younger. So every month I'll go online and listen to a current Top 40 playlist to hear what is popular at the moment. I'll check out what movies people are watching and download one from time to time. I'll also check out entertainment websites and follow some celebrities on social media just to stay up to date.

Why should you become a student of culture? Simple. People who don't understand today's culture will never be able to speak into it. Whether you agree with the culture or not, understanding it is a prerequisite to being able to influence it.

4. Surround Yourself with Younger People

Another way to make sure you stay relevant is to have younger people in your life. If you're a parent, don't just hang out with your kids; explore their world and take a keen interest in it. Try to understand them rather than just criticize them. Similarly, at work, whenever you build a team, make sure you invite and include young adults into the mix.

One of the most refreshing things about the teams I've led is that they've always had younger leaders on board—sometimes *very* young leaders. The temptation is to want to teach them everything you've learned, and that's great when you can do it in a way that's welcomed by them. But one of the best ways to earn the affection and buy-in of a younger team is to listen as much as you speak, to learn as much as you attempt to teach. You can learn so much from younger leaders, and they hold the key to your organization's renewal and future, in terms of both personnel and ideas.

The Gift of Aging Well

What do you do with all your accumulated life experience? It's true that you can be wise at any age, but there's something about reaching age forty that allows wisdom to blossom if you nurture it well. I still have much to learn, but when I entered my forties, it was like new sequences started firing in my brain, aligning insights in a way that suddenly began to make sense of things previously mysterious to me. I began to see patterns in people's lives and in their character that I hadn't seen before. Life started to seem a lot less random and haphazard.

That's one of the benefits of getting older. You see things you just couldn't see at age twenty. My forties were the decade when I started writing more widely, building into my team and outside leaders, and guiding young leaders as they entered the workforce. It's the decade I was able to apply much of what I had learned to my teaching at our church and to my own life. Accumulated life experiences and insight gave a refreshing new depth to my reading of Scripture. The Christian Scriptures have always rung true to me, but in my forties I really began to realize *why* they rang true.

The best years for leaders who are able to communicate with the culture often seem to happen somewhere between age forty-five and seventy-five. If you don't navigate these years well, these are also the years where irrelevance accelerates. But if you pay attention to the things we've discussed, these can be not only your peak earning years but also your peak contributing years. That's what relevance allows you to do. Earlier I mentioned author and scholar Dallas Willard, who died in 2013 at age seventy-five. He contributed as much in his last two decades as in his first five decades. When Dr. Willard passed away, I was saddened because he was a voice I wanted to hear from for years to come.

So many people do their best work and craft their greatest contributions later in life. They give a lifetime of knowledge, insight, and wisdom back to the culture. Instead of railing against the way things are, they leverage the past and present to make the future better.

Think about it. You have older people—authors, actors, artists, musicians, friends, family—you adore. And you're not worried about their age. They've bridged the communication gap between their generation and yours, between their preferred culture and today's culture. In fact, their stage of life might be the very reason they add so much value to so many people. Their years offer wisdom that youth simply can't access.

Growing older does not necessarily mean growing irrelevant. In fact, staying relevant to the culture around you may be the gateway into your best years yet.

GET READY FOR A SURPRISE: TRANSFORMATION

You know that change isn't easy at all, and there's something deep inside you that will keep resisting it. That's understandable. But what happens when you resist the status quo, embrace radical ideas and approaches, study the culture, and surround yourself with younger people? Change becomes familiar. It becomes a way of life.

At first change feels strange, difficult, and foreign. And to some extent, those feelings never go away. But something profound happens if you stick with change and decide you're not going to stop evolving. Eventually, change becomes transformation. It won't happen right away, but after a number of years (most frequently, between five and seven), you'll realize that you've been transformed. You're no longer who you were.

The difference between change and transformation is powerful. On the outside, they look similar. Looking at a person who's changed versus one who's been transformed, you won't see a big *external* difference. But inside, the transformed person is *significantly* different. What's happened? The transformed person no longer wants to go back to the way things were. Unlike the story of Moses and the Israelites, the slaves no longer want to go back to Egypt. When true transformation occurs, the person embraces the future more than the past.

The key to seeing transformation take root is to keep changing, keep experimenting, keep risking. You won't feel the shift immediately, but at some point you'll wake up and realize you don't want things to be the way they used to be. You'll begin to feel that "the good old days" should be left behind and that your best days are ahead of you. And that ushers in hope, excitement, and joy.

Unimplemented Change Becomes Regret

A final thought on this topic: the change you don't implement often becomes something none of us wants—regret.

People who fail to undertake change usually look back and yearn for what might have been. You probably already have a few of those examples in your life. The job you could have taken but waited too long to decide on—regret. The girl you should have asked out but never found the nerve to chat with—regret. The stock you knew you should have bought but didn't—regret. That apology you should have made to your dad before he died—deep regret.

Change is hard, but the right kind ushers in so much good. You may prefer to do things your way and keep everything the same. But for the sake of the next generation, for the sake of contributing meaningfully throughout your entire life, don't just *intend* to change. Actually do it. Because unimplemented change will become regret.

PART V

PRIDE

IT'S NOT JUST
THE NARCISSISTS

How Pride Gets the Best of Us

A few years ago, I embarked on a twelve-month spending fast. I had been inspired by my assistant, Sarah Piercy, who decided she would not spend discretionary money on herself for a year. I can spend with the best of them, and my appetite for more seems to be a constant in my life. So I thought a year of no discretionary spending would be a good thing for me.

My basic rules included no new clothes (only secondhand), no new technology (that part was *hard*), and no new optional items; in addition, all gift cards I received had to be given away or spent to benefit others. Maybe my favorite question to emerge out of my spending fast was from people who asked, "So did you buy any food?" No, actually I didn't eat or drink anything for an entire year. (Of course, I bought food!)

Three months into my fast, I was about an hour from home, heading to an appointment, when the hot tea I had been sipping slipped out of my hand. This wasn't a little spill. My pants were *soaked*. It was like an invisible hand reached over and poured the liquid all over my clothes. The stain was effectively placed to make me look like I'd been unable to reach the bathroom in time or perhaps like I had slept on the streets for a few weeks. I immediately thought, *I have a meeting. I need to go buy a new pair of pants. This definitely qualifies as an exception to my spending fast. I can't wear pants that are badly stained. There's no other alternative.*

Providentially, I drove past a Walmart, so I turned into the parking lot. Parking my car, I started debating with myself. It went like this:

"You could wear those pants, you know. They're just stained."

"No, that would be embarrassing. I would never dress like that."

"And they are, after all, really stained. If you bought the pants at Walmart, that doesn't even qualify as breaking a spending fast, right? Walmart is not the place where you normally go to buy clothes. It's not like you're breaking any rules anyway."

"So what's really driving this, Carey? Basically, you want to protect your image. You're too embarrassed to be the guy with the big stain in an awkward location. And now you're an elitist about Walmart because you're too stylish to shop for clothes there."

"Shut up, self."

Do you see how pride shows up? I mean, none of us wants to be seen in public with stained pants. We're afraid we'll be judged, dismissed, or humiliated. Nobody wants to be looked down on. We have reputations to protect and images to project, even at Walmart.

Worse, I had blogged just the day before about how I had successfully completed the first quarter of my spending fast and hadn't broken one rule. Now I was rewriting the rules in my head so I could claim I hadn't cheated. See what pride does?

Pride pushed me through the door of Walmart. But as I walked in, I became even more conflicted and then increasingly convicted. I relented. Instead of going to the men's clothing section, I went to the men's restroom.

Fortunately, I spotted one of those turbo dryers mounted on the wall. I used my hands to scoop lots of water onto the affected pant leg and crotch area. If anyone thought I might have wet my pants before, I had just removed all doubt. My pants were now drenched. Brilliant.

I spent ten minutes at the automatic hand dryer, twisting and turning to get my pants dry. To make matters more interesting, the dryer was positioned slightly outside the door, giving customers at several checkout lines a front-row view. Awesome. The stain largely disappeared, and I left the store mostly dry.

My lesson that day? I got back into my car realizing how proud I am. I really didn't want to be seen with dirty clothes, let alone leave anyone with the impression I'd become incontinent. I was afraid people would judge me or think less of me. I didn't have the humility to risk being misunderstood, judged, or seen as uncool, not even for an hour until I was able to get back home.

Pride runs so deep. It's one of the cardinal sins against God. Pride made me believe these things:

- What other people think matters more than what God thinks.
- His love for me is not enough.
- His approval of me is inadequate unless I have the approval of others.
- Appearances count for a lot.
- I am what others think I am.

Deep down, the experience revealed that I think I'm not enough, that my clothes have to make a statement about me because I'm not capable of making a statement on my own. I fully realize we're a civilized people who wear reasonably fashionable clothes, but there's something deeper than that underneath, isn't there?

HE'S SO VAIN

It's so easy to spot pride. Okay, let me try that again. It's so easy to spot pride in *other people*. There, that's far more accurate. You see pride all the time. You know people who are too proud to ask for advice, even though they desperately need it. You see people who cling to their ways, even when they're bad ways, because they're too proud to change. You know people who are always one-upping others, people who love to go on and on about all their accomplishments. You know people who brag about everything they've acquired, achieved, and experienced, like their fifth vacation in the last year that you heard all about despite never inquiring. You know far too many people who are obsessed with themselves whether or not there's much to be obsessed with.

How do you become that person? How do you become the one others secretly roll their eyes at, the one who makes people cringe, the one no one wants to listen to? How do you become the person who's chiefly self-focused?

Pride disguises itself in many ways. It's so pervasive that it has to be subtle. If it knew only one form, we'd stop it dead in its tracks. So it spawns. Pride morphs, and it creeps in using methods that often go unnoticed. Let me get the most obvious form out of the way right now so we can focus on what likely afflicts you and me. The most obvious form of pride is narcissism, which is an issue for some people but not most. How do you know if you're in that category? Narcissists really do think they're God's gift to humanity. They demand to be the center of attention; they dominate conversations, interrupt people, think they're better, have to stay on top at all costs, can't celebrate the success of others, and always have an excuse if they're not first. They're obsessed with themselves because they think they're oh so awesome.

If that's you, let me save you some time. Go get help. Serious help. See a Christian counselor, talk to a professional, and check yourself into a clinic.

Now, on to the rest of us. You're probably not a raging egomaniac or a diagnosed narcissist, but does that mean pride hasn't snagged you? Strangely, most of us don't see ourselves as proud, yet many of us are. It should be no surprise that pride runs deep, because pride is, in many ways, the master sin. It's the root of our rebellion against God, against others, and even against what's best for us.

Pride at its heart is an obsession with self. It generates the desire you feel to protect, project, manipulate, jockey, advance, pretend, inflate, and brag. It's so pervasive that, as Benjamin Franklin observed, if you ever reached the point of becoming humble, you might find yourself wanting to boast about how meek you are. Pride is the hallmark of fools as well. Foolishness is simply unapplied knowledge. Fools know; they just don't care. They've figured it out. Their way is better, and if they end up in the ditch, well, it wasn't their fault. Just leave them alone.

Pride, as we'll see, even lives in the hearts of the insecure—people who aren't sure they're all that great and secretly doubt they ever will be. Honestly, pride shows up *all over the place* in our lives, and every time it does, it's deadly.

WHAT PRIDE KILLS

So why pay attention to pride? Unaddressed, pride will destroy many of the things you care about or know you should care about. It will leave a trail of destruction strewn with things you used to value or that a better version of you would treasure. Pride will snuff out your empathy, stifle your compassion, create division, suffocate love, foster jealousy, deaden your soul, and make you think all this is normal. It can turn you into the kind of person you loathe. Even if doesn't do that, it will infect your relationships with a toxin that may not be fatal but is poisonous enough to ruin your joy.

In many ways, pride is related to everything else covered in this book. Pride will lead to cynicism and accelerate burnout. It will leave you feeling disconnected and can cause you to become irrelevant. And by the time it has run its course, pride will leave you feeling empty, despite everything you've accomplished. Pride will cost you friendships, intimacy, respect, lost opportunities, rest, peace of mind, wisdom, and even money. It's hard to imagine the stakes being much higher.

IT'S NOT JUST EGOMANIACS WHO ARE PRIDEFUL

The biggest challenge with pride is that for most of us, it's everywhere. Sure, you don't spend most of your day thinking you're great; you spend most of your day with a gnawing sense that you're not. But that, too, can lead to an obsession with self. That self-obsession is another way to invite pride to run right through the middle of your soul. This is a threat I often face in my life.

I find pride shows up everywhere, even in the least likely of places. Like at Walmart when it appeared I'd peed my pants. If I'm honest with myself, it turns out I'm a bit obsessed with cars that are ultraclean, grass that is mowed in diamond patterns, and a workspace that is uncluttered and attractive. Some of that is healthy. Some of it isn't healthy at all. Personally, I think my wife looks great without lipstick or makeup, but she feels a little insecure heading into public without it. I don't get that because I love her as she is. But I realized a long time ago that my clean car is her lipstick. I suspect if I show up in a mudmobile, people will think less of me.

Is it possible that pride emerges out of a place of insecurity? Absolutely. In fact, for most of us, that's exactly where it breeds.

SIGNS INSECURITY IS DRIVING YOUR PRIDE

Pride sneaks in even among the insecure and drives a wedge between who *we* think we are and who *God* thinks we are. How do you know if your insecurity—your sense that you don't measure up—is driving an unhealthy focus on yourself? Here are five signs I've recognized that I hope can help you.

1. You Compare Yourself to Others

Ever find yourself comparing yourself to other people? Of course you do; you're human.

You and I have lots to learn from other people, but insecure people aren't driven so much by a desire to *learn* as they are by the desire to know whether they are better or worse than others. There is a world of difference between tracking with others to grow, learn, empathize, or celebrate versus tracking with others to see how you stack up. One is fundamentally healthy, the other, destructive. There's a lot of sin involved with comparison.

Want to see how twisted this is? Sure, maybe you don't feel great about yourself. But you tell yourself as a source of comfort that at least you're not as bad off as some other people. So pride compels you to pick out people to convince yourself you're superior. You may not have your dream body, but at least you're not as heavy as that certain coworker. You're no PhD, but gosh, you're smarter than most of the people in your class. You're not driving a BMW, but your car isn't as dented and scratched as your brother-in-law's. You select people who, in your mind, assure you that you're brighter, richer, faster, or more attractive. My counselor has a great name for this: *compar-rogance*. It's the arrogance born of comparison.

The fact that you might be afflicted by this condition should come as no surprise. Virtually every ad you've ever seen was designed to do two things: first, convince you that your life does not stack up favorably to the general population, and second, persuade you that whatever X Company is offering you will make your life so much better. You'll totally go from inferior to superior as soon as you get the new product or service. And it will stay that way until, of course, the company releases a new version, which will mean the one you just bought is badly outdated and you, in case you were wondering, are once again inadequate. The cycle is insidious.

2. Your Self-Worth Is Determined by Your Latest Performance

This is a challenge for all of us who are driven by results, which would clearly include me. I'm addicted to progress. If things aren't moving up and moving on, I become alarmed quickly. In some ways that approach to life is good, and in some ways it can warp your sense of security. One sure sign of insecurity is that your opinion of yourself rises and falls with how you perform or what others say about you. Your identity should be more secure than your latest results, but for many of us, it's not.

How do you know whether you've tethered your identity to your performance? As Tim Keller put it, "When work is your identity, success goes to your head, and failure goes to your heart."[1] Or if work isn't your particular poison, then substitute whatever else you've tied to your identity; you'll likewise discover that success goes to your head and failure to your heart.

Some of you might object and ask whether this means people should just throw up their hands and give up. After all, progress makes life better. But there's a big difference between taking things seriously and taking things personally. Secure people take issues seriously; they just don't take them personally anymore. They realize that who they are and what they do are separate things.

3. You Can't Celebrate Someone Else's Success

Insecure people struggle with celebration. They have a hard time celebrating their own progress because they are never sure they have done well enough. And they have difficulty celebrating the accomplishments of another because someone else's success threatens them. The pie isn't large enough for everyone to get a fair slice.

If you're insecure, someone else's victory means your loss, with the opposite also applying. It's a zero-sum game. If someone else does well, you can't help but wonder why you didn't see the same results, or you feel like the odds are stacked against you. Because you feel bad about yourself, you can't feel good about others. Once again, insecurity has led you to focus on yourself to the exclusion of others.

4. You Squeeze Gifted People Out of Your Life

Pride doesn't make room for the gifting of others. You'll find yourself drifting away from your highly successful sister in family settings, not wanting to engage her in conversation beyond "Hello." You'll be drawn to friends who are less achieving than you are so that you end up with the best stories and feel superior by comparison. Or if your social circle does include others who have accomplished more than you, you will find yourself deeply envious of them and critical of them behind their backs. Proud people always feel a need to be the most talented or skilled. As a result, the number of gifted people around them is much lower than it is around people who are secure and less obsessed with themselves.

Ask yourself, *How comfortable am I around people I think are better than me, even at the things I'm good at?* That will give you a fair measure of your security. One sign of humble people is the ability to attract and keep people more gifted and competent than themselves for the sake of their team or cause.

5. You Want Some Say in Everything

Proud people end up being controlling people. If insecurity drives you, you'll always want to add your little bit of knowledge, insight, or even an anecdote to everyone else's story. It won't feel complete if the other person gets the spotlight and you get overlooked. You may even tend to be a know-it-all, whether you really are knowledgeable or are just making stuff up to trump others in the conversation. Know-it-alls weren't much fun in kindergarten; they are less fun in the adult world.

The truth is most of us are talented or even knowledgeable in only one or two areas. Even then, you became that way through the help, encouragement, and assistance of other people. When you value the counsel and input of others, especially on the things you're best at, you embark on a path toward greater wisdom.

SEE THE SIGNS?

Now that we've rooted out less obvious signs of pride, do you see any of them brooding within you? Most of us don't see pride coming because it morphs into subtle forms. The subtleties don't always lead us to being large and in charge, but they keep us up at night and stressed all day. They keep us worried that we're not enough and haven't got what it takes. They keep us afraid to fail, afraid to be honest, and worried about being seen for who we really are. Pride has worked its way into the mix because, once again, it's made us obsessed with ourselves.

So what is pride doing? What is the logical extension? If we let pride run its course, untamed and spawning, what is the result? Left unchecked and unaddressed, pride leads to a hardened heart.

Pride Hardens Your Heart

Let pride run its course, and it will deaden your heart. Pride inoculates you from the counsel of others and the stirrings of your conscience. It makes you think that the rules don't apply to you or that you can violate them without repercussion.

If you've ever read the Old Testament—the part of Scripture that chronicles the story of God's people before Jesus came along—you know that the condition of the human heart is a recurring theme. The more often I read the passages about hardness of heart, the more nervous I become. That's because it seems to be such a common condition.

David was one of the greatest kings who ever ruled the nation of Israel. He transitioned the people of Israel from a ragtag group of former refugees who were starting to become a nation into a global superpower. And, from all we can tell, he did it while keeping a pure and supple heart. We know that not just because certain writers describe David's heart as being open but also because we have his journal (found in the book of Psalms). There we can see the interior life of a man whose heart longed after God. Until, apparently, David reached the height of his power.

One afternoon, David strolled on his rooftop when he should have been in battle with his troops. He spotted a gorgeous woman bathing. Turned out she was married, and her husband was where David should've been: fighting with the army. Evidently, David didn't care. He summoned this woman, Bathsheba, seduced her, and got her pregnant.

To cover up the immoral act, David called Bathsheba's husband, Uriah, back from battle so he could go home and, presumably, have sex with his wife. This would make it look like Uriah, not David, was the father. Except Uriah had more integrity than the king. He wouldn't go home and sleep with his wife while his country was at war. So he slept outside the palace.

When David heard about this, he panicked. The next day he decided to get Uriah drunk, thinking an inebriated Uriah would want to do what almost any guy with a few drinks in him might do: go home and proposition his bride. Except he wouldn't, not while his friends were in battle.

Finally, David concluded that the only option left was to have Uriah killed. He ordered his commander to send Uriah to the front lines, where death was likely. Just collateral damage—you know how these things go. And sure enough, during an intense battle Uriah was killed. No longer would he be around to expose the truth or express outrage. In a final twist of irony, David took Bathsheba home to be his wife.

You know what contributed to that horrible story? Pride. The leader who did things right far more than he did them wrong let his heart grow hard at the zenith of his power. He stopped caring, stopped submitting, stopped believing he was under the law, and started following his unfiltered desires. His heart had lost its suppleness.

David went from being one of the wisest people of his era to acting the fool. He knew better, but something inside him cracked. The things that normally touched his heart or pricked his conscience no longer did. And that's how the death spiral starts.

If you study David's life before his actions with Bathsheba and then afterward, you see a man whose life was never the same again. Not only did he and Bathsheba lose their baby, but his whole family seemed to careen into a tailspin. Division, treason, and even rape began to taint David's family line. Someone who used to seek God's heart began to seek his own, and the fallout was tragic.

Throughout Scripture, we see God wanting to do so much more in the lives of his people, but he couldn't because their hearts were hard. You probably don't want that to be your fate. Which begs the question, What exactly does a hard heart look like? Glad you asked. There are at least four characteristics to watch for.

1. Superior

A proud and hardened heart makes you feel superior to others (notice this crops up all over the place when you're proud?). Maybe you're not the best, but you dress a little better, went to a better college, have a slightly nicer house, and had an exotic vacation *they* didn't have. No, you're not the greatest, but you think you're better than the dollar-store crowd or your cousin with the rusted-out clunker in his side yard. You can't help but scoff at the guy on the scooter who's clearly eaten too much in his fifty-odd years.

See how ugly superiority gets? Your pride and insecurity need you to be better than somebody—anybody. You drift toward superiority because your inferiority has taken you there.

2. Judgmental

A judgmental attitude springs directly from the noxious well of superiority because to stay ahead, you have to invent reasons why others are behind. To bolster your sense of success, tenuous as it is, you concoct explanations for why you're better than everyone else. It's too bad your colleague is facing tough times, but if he worked harder and hustled like you do, well, things would go better for him.

It's sad that the woman in your book group can't seem to lose weight, but you're pretty sure she's not living off kale and coconut oil. There must be empty cartons of ice cream in her trash can. If you ate that much, you'd be her size too.

You look down on your weed-smoking neighbor because you would never do that kind of thing (so you tell yourself as you savor your sixteen-ounce steak and those amazing sweet potato fries). After all, self-righteous Christians don't do drugs. They do food.

3. Unaccountable

A hardened heart will also help you justify avoiding real accountability. You can be creative in how you do that.

Sometimes pride will make you decide you're accountable to no one. You stop listening to your spouse, kids, friends, coworkers, or boss. If you read Scripture or other works that suggest what you're doing is wrong, you create a tidy rationale for why your situation is different or why the text doesn't apply to you.

Alternatively, pride might have you surround yourself with people who tell you what you want to hear. They never challenge you, never speak up, and never present hard truth. Or maybe you've gradually eliminated all those with an opposing point of view. They disagreed with you, so why would you hang out with them?

Unrestrained, pride will relentlessly drive you to remove whatever challenges it, and one of its most consistent threats is accountability.

4. Isolated

Ultimately pride leads you to a very strange space. You think your bragging and devotion to your own success make you better in the eyes of others when they are doing exactly the opposite.

The only person your pride impresses is you. Nobody else is attracted to your arrogance or self-absorption. Other people will peel off from you as quickly as they can, or maybe they'll tolerate you because they have to. You're their dad, after all, or they work for or with you. But they are motivated to spend zero extra time with you. You may spend your entire life building your kingdom, but just know this: a life devoted to self ultimately leaves you alone. That's exactly where pride leaves you: isolated.

PRIDE CAN BE SCANDALOUS

It won't take long to bring to mind politicians and business leaders who let their success go to their heads and were felled by pride. Leaders get ousted by boards because they won't listen or get caught breaking the rules. Politicians get defeated because they're seen as out of touch or entitled.

But pride doesn't just topple leaders; it infects all of us. If a pastor makes the headlines these days, it's usually because he or she engaged in an illicit affair or embezzled money. Usually, but not always. There have been sobering accounts recently of more than a few large-church pastors who struggled with pride. Scott Thumma, a Hartford Seminary sociologist, made a great point about why pride is a particular issue for church leaders: "My sense is that many of the celebrity religious leaders are well aware of and intentionally attempt to guard themselves against sexual and financial temptations. But they forget that pride comes before a fall."[2]

To his credit, well-known Christian pastor and author John Piper gave a painful explanation for the eight-month sabbatical he took from ministry, publicly stating, "My soul, my marriage, my family, and my ministry-pattern need a reality check from the Holy Spirit." He wrote that he noticed "several species of pride in my soul that, while they may not rise to the level of disqualifying me for ministry, grieve me,"[3] so he took a sabbatical to deal with the root issues. A year later, Piper clarified that his time off had been dedicated to addressing his "characteristic sins," including "selfishness, anger, self-pity, quickness to blame, and sullenness."[4] Piper demonstrated so much humility, honesty, and integrity in doing what he did. Personally, I can relate to every one of Piper's struggles and have recognized them at different times in my own life. My guess is you have too. As my wife said to me, "Maybe we should all resign. There's a sense in which maybe those who have stepped back have done the honorable thing, isn't there?"

This is where pride can take you. You and I may not be well known enough for our problems to make headlines, but our pride is making headlines in our homes and with the people closest to us. Your spouse and kids feel the full weight of your pride, whether it expresses itself in foolish decisions for which your family pays the price, hardness of heart that shuts them out, or judgmental superiority that makes you hard to live with.

So how do you battle your pride, that ugly thing you've spotted in yourself and that I've definitely seen in myself? How do you make sure you don't end up with a story you don't want to tell? Start by cultivating humility, which is where our discussion takes us next.

10

HABITS OF THE HUMBLE

Only Humility Will Get You Out of What Pride Got You Into

Pride is insidious, creeping up on you uninvited and unnoticed. Take my experience with travel, for example. Until my honeymoon, I had traveled by airplane only once. And even after our honeymoon, we rarely flew anywhere. It was too expensive. As a result, for years, on the rare occasion we flew somewhere, I was grateful to be on the plane. A bit thrilled, to be honest.

But as I started speaking at conferences and events, things slowly changed. I began to notice that not all seats are created equal, and being over six feet tall, I thought I needed a better row and seat position. Once I discovered that, it wasn't long until I discovered that an aisle seat on a bulkhead row was even better than on an exit row. *It helps,* I told myself, *when you're my height, to have a little extra legroom.*

Then I flew business class for the first time. It was a free upgrade I didn't even ask for. The flight attendant called me by name. The seats were wide and supple, with enough legroom for even an NBA player. The food was free and delicious. Upgrades like that are the gateway drugs of a frequent flyer wired the way I am.

My new life of luxury was cut sadly short. After that first business-class flight, I boarded my next flight to discover I was in the *back row.* But it was worse than that. I was in the back-row *middle* seat. If you fly even a little bit, you know there is nothing in the world worse than a middle seat. You have elbow wars on both sides of you, fighting for a little armrest space. At least one of your seatmates will probably lean onto you at some point in the flight or will ignore the fact that you have headphones on and try to talk to you . . . for hours.

I couldn't believe how upset I was. I had zero gratitude, only resentment. I wanted to write a blog post called "Five Things That Stink When You're in a Back-Row Middle Seat." I started texting my assistant, Sarah, begging to know how on earth I ended up in row 35 and complaining like a toddler.

Somebody should have stuck a pacifier in my mouth that day. I deserved it.

I'd become accustomed to status and rank, and, worse, I felt like I was owed it. Pride convinced me I deserved more. The problem with success (even a small bit of it) is that you get addicted to all the trappings. And pride will convince you that you are entitled to it all.

How do you tame the raging beast of pride in all its forms?

Through humility.

Nothing kills pride like humility does. Only humility can get you out of what pride got you into.

So how do you become more humble? It's not like you can just wake up one morning and say, "Self, today be humble" and then have a day characterized by saintlike meekness. It would be great if it worked that way, but I've never been able to pull it off. Instead, humility can be found in three ways.

I suppose the easiest way would be to cultivate humility as a discipline or habit from a young age, but it's rare for that to ever happen. For most of us, it's far more painful than that. If humility has been part of your character from childhood, congratulations. But now on to the rest of us.

A second possible (but not desirable) way to learn humility is actually through humiliation. To be humiliated is to *be* humbled, not by your own choice, but by circumstances or by another person. Being fired from your job or declaring bankruptcy or getting dumped by a friend or having a giant stain on your pants at Walmart are all potentially humiliating experiences. Anytime you feel embarrassment, humiliation and pride are lurking in the wings. Humiliation, by definition, is *involuntary* humility. It comes to you when it's the last thing you want. When you've fallen flat on your face on the floor, you can't go much lower. You can't really fall off the floor. You've been *brought* low, which is the essence of the idea behind the virtue of humility. Except you didn't *choose* to be there. You were forced there. The danger with humiliation is not in the *act* of being humiliated. No, the danger is that humility is easily abandoned. You can brush it off as soon as you brush yourself off. It's far too easy to get up and walk away not only from the embarrassment but from all the lessons you could have learned from it. Most of us want to put as much distance between us and humiliation as possible as quickly as we can. Humility stays only if you invite it. Even more than that, you need to submit to it, crave it, hone it, develop it, and nurture it. Otherwise it leaves, and pride returns as soon as the bruises on your knees heal.

That leads us to the third and perhaps most universal way humility arrives and stays: you invite it and cultivate it. You learn the ways of the humble, and you make it your principal way of operating. If that happens, then pride doesn't have any room to stay, let alone grow. This is a difficult process because humility is never attractive to the people who need it most. Pride looks far more appealing. But think about it: pride looks attractive only to the proud. You don't like proud people, but you love the humble. It's like pride and humility are part of some perverse inverted mirror. What you need most (humility) looks singularly unattractive, but what others hate in you (pride) looks downright appealing.

Which is why humility really needs to be embraced, developed, and valued to take root in your life. So how do you do that? How do you cultivate humility? You'd be tempted to think it's an attitude, and to some extent it is. But cultivating an attitude of humility is hard because you're dealing with intangibles.

So how do you know you're humble? Monitor your actions in key areas I'll describe next. The humble act differently than the proud do. If you adopt the action, the attitude may well follow. And even if your heart continues to be a mix of pride and humility, your actions will demonstrate humility to the people around you.

I've had to learn the hard way (and the people around me have the bumps and bruises to prove it), but here are some practices that will help you cultivate and practice humility.

Never Lose Your Gratitude

Remember when you put something on your Christmas list when you were a kid and actually got what you wanted? I had that experience when I got a little orange tractor one year. I was over the moon.

You were often grateful as a kid largely because you didn't have the ability to get anything yourself. You knew you didn't have the means. That went for something as simple as enjoying an ice-cream cone on a hot summer day or being able to order the large fries if you went out for dinner. You were grateful because you knew you were dependent on other people's acts of kindness.

When did that start to change? For most of us, purchasing power arrived with our first job. I remember buying my first record at thirteen when I had some money of my own. I was grateful and excited because finally I could go to the record store and buy my own albums.

But buying your first record is different from buying your eleventh. Having ten dollars to your name is pretty exciting when it's your first ten dollars. But having thirteen dollars in the bank in high school when you're living amid three milk crates of vinyl records is a different feeling. The more you have, the easier it is to lose your gratitude. Scarcity creates gratitude, and most of us live in relative abundance, globally speaking.

Another factor creeps in as well. When you're thirty-five years old, rather than five years old, you've got some skin in the game. You hustled. You worked long hours. You finished college when others dropped out. You saved for a down payment on a house. You didn't blow your money or your future at a casino. You were responsible.

And as a result, you begin to think you earned what you have. Maybe you even think you deserve it. When I feel that way, I force myself to acknowledge that everything I have is a gift from God. That includes the mind I'm leveraging to craft these words as I write, the breath I'm breathing that will keep me alive to the next sentence (God willing), the keyboard I'm typing on, and the vacation I just took. He enables me to have all these things. God has graciously provided. And honestly, my faith convinces me he didn't intend for everything he has given me to be solely for my personal benefit. My faith tells me God has given me everything I have so I can share it and use it to benefit others.

Even though I'm in a season where my life, by most accounts, has gone well, it would be ridiculous for me to claim full credit. I'm not sure I can claim credit for the people who read my words or listen to me give a talk or download podcasts I host. People ask me all the time how I built an audience, and to be sure, I can outline a few principles. But the truth is, there's *mystery* in it. There's *grace* in it. There's a providential element in it that I don't fully understand and that I certainly didn't produce myself. The best business leaders will articulate the same thing. They may talk about hard work and determination, but the great leaders will also often talk about luck or chance. They realize they're not as smart as their success makes them appear. What they call luck I call providence. So much grace has flowed through my life. Frankly, it's easy to ignore unless I *decide* (intentionally) to never lose my gratitude. I'm sure the same is true for you. Gratitude fosters humility because it moves you out of the role of the star in your story.

So how do you make sure you never lose your gratitude? First, express your thankfulness regularly. If you pray, offer prayers of gratitude. Second, fall more in love with the Giver than you ever do with his gifts. Third, never claim full credit for your story. Acknowledge the role of grace and providence publicly when you talk.

What are you grateful for? Here's a better question: What *should* you be grateful for?

Take the Low Place

What exactly does it mean to take the low place? For most of us, we remember when we had nothing. Think back to when you were a student or starting out on your own. You lived on ramen noodles. You rode the bus, dreaming of the day you'd own a beater. There wasn't much pretense to you because, well, there was nothing to brag about or even grow attached to.

If you've experienced success at work, you've noticed your lifestyle improving a little. Maybe a lot. First it was a nice cubicle all to yourself. Then maybe a small expense account. Next it was an office. Then a nice office. Soon you were getting great tickets to the game, with reserved parking. You realized you love any VIP status that comes your way.

Proud leaders enjoy titles, corner offices, and the praise and perks that come with a position. The proud take the high place. They always want something better and more.

The humble, by contrast, take the low place, intent on serving rather than being served. They shake off titles and don't mind washing the dishes or sweeping the floor. They're happy to take out the trash or offer someone their seat on the bus or subway. They volunteer for the grunt work, the projects no one else wants to do. Nothing is below them when they adopt a humble stance.

Taking the low place doesn't mean you will always occupy a low-level position at work or in other endeavors. On the contrary, humble people are often recognized and rewarded for their gracious hearts and diligent service. So what do you do with perks if they come to you? Maybe you do have a decent office, nice car, or lake house. Perhaps you get front-of-the-line status because you're on the road so much. Here's a simple discipline: *share them*. If God has blessed you, that's wonderful. But surely he didn't intend for those blessings to benefit you alone. Share them with others, especially with those who don't have what you do.

OPEN YOUR NOTEBOOK

Unchecked, pride will blind you. You'll stop learning from anyone you deem to be beneath you or equal to you. You'll snicker to yourself when someone offers you advice. You'll think, *What does he know about that?* or *Who's she to give anyone advice?*

Pride fueled by insecurity prevents an attitude of teachability and an openness to guidance. You'll stop learning from people you think are smarter than you or more successful than you. Jealousy kills learning and shuts down instructive conversations.

Humility is not like that. It learns from anyone, anywhere. It keeps its notebook open. That may take the form of a physical notebook, or it might simply mean you take notes on your phone. Whatever your method, take notes when you have lunch with someone, attend a class, or listen to a talk. Glean insights from others.

Are you always going to be surrounded by brilliant people? Of course not. But that doesn't mean you can't learn something. So keep your mind open and your pen handy, regardless of whom you're meeting with. And especially when you're with someone you're envious of or someone you think you're better than. Humility always keeps its notebook open.

PUSH OTHER PEOPLE INTO THE SPOTLIGHT

Pride wants to be acknowledged, recognized, and celebrated. Sometimes pride will have you believing you deserve it. Sometimes it will convince you you've been overlooked and the world should recognize the treasure that is you.

As a result, pride hogs the spotlight as much as it can. Want me to give a talk? You bet. Need me to lead the meeting? No problem. Want me to head up that next project? Of course. Want to give me an opportunity to shine? Yep, I'm there. Inside your head, pride is saying, *Finally, someone sees how valuable I really am. After all, I'm so talented and I've worked so hard; why would they give this to anyone else?* If insecurity is driving your obsession with self, pride might make you think, *Look, it took me so long to get here, if I don't grab this I might never get another chance. Ever. And I'd better not let other people in on it in case they see they're now smarter than I am.*

Humility doesn't think or act that way at all. It willingly pushes other people into the spotlight. It's never jealous. It delights in the success of others. In fact, sometimes humble people even enjoy others' success more than their own success. Humility is like that.

Paradoxically, pushing other people into the spotlight is one of the best forms of job security. If you can produce leaders who are as good as or better than you, pretty much any organization will hire you instantly. Helping others succeed and sharing the stage with them doesn't make you less valuable; it makes you more valuable. When you're humble, you realize the overall mission is more important than you are.

Not confident you're ready to push other people into the spotlight? Some advice: start before you feel you're ready. If the voice inside your head is screaming messages of jealousy and insecurity, push others into the spotlight anyway. Celebrate their successes publicly. When you do, you drive a silver spike into the heart of pride. Pushing others into the spotlight breaks the stranglehold of envy (and even fear) in your life.

GET RIDICULOUSLY HONEST WITH YOURSELF (AND GOD)

Pride is like a weed, and humility is like your lawn. Weeds need pretty much no fertilizer or water to grow; they just show up and effortlessly take over. Your lawn needs to be fertilized, aerated, watered, and nurtured to stand a chance of healthy growth.

One of the best ways to win the war against pride is to get ridiculously honest with yourself and with God. Check your motives constantly. Pray about them. Ask other people for a reality check (sometimes they see motivations you're blind to). If you feel a hint of selfishness, confess it and lay the ugliness out before God.

If you're in the habit of reading the Bible, have you ever had times when you weren't reading Scripture but Scripture was reading you? I had one of those moments a few years ago when I was reading a passage in the New Testament.

This passage in the book of James stopped me dead in my tracks. It described exactly what I was experiencing in that moment. Read through it and see what you feel:

> If you are wise and understand God's ways, prove it by living an honorable life, doing good works with the humility that comes from wisdom. But if you are bitterly jealous and there is selfish ambition in your heart, don't cover up the truth with boasting and lying. For jealousy and selfishness are not God's kind of wisdom. Such things are earthly, unspiritual, and demonic. For wherever there is jealousy and selfish ambition, there you will find disorder and evil of every kind.
>
>   But the wisdom from above is first of all pure. It is also peace loving, gentle at all times, and willing to yield to others. It is full of mercy and the fruit of good deeds. It shows no favoritism and is always sincere. And those who are peacemakers will plant seeds of peace and reap a harvest of righteousness.[1]

When I read that passage one morning a few years back, it wrecked me. Owned me. Convicted me. Why? Because it described exactly what I was feeling—not the holy part in verses 17–18 but the terrible part in verses 14–16 that basically said my emotions were aligned with the devil.

At that time, I felt jealous of another leader I suspected was a better speaker than I was. I had allowed it to eat me up. I felt selfish, insecure, and did *not* want to share the spotlight any more than I had to. Pride grew ugly things in my heart, things that were not from God at all. They were the opposite of what God offers.

Instead of blowing the passage off and ignoring it, I admitted that it described me. I confessed it. I didn't want those words to characterize me, but I knew without a doubt that they did. Instead of moving on, the next day I went back to the same text, praying as I read through it again. I didn't leave those six verses until the repugnant things they described relinquished their grip on my heart. It took more than a week.

Every time I've read that text in the years since then, I have stopped and thanked God for what he dealt with inside me during that season. I'm so grateful. But you don't get to that kind of breakthrough without brutal honesty about what's really going on.

What do you need to be ridiculously honest about with yourself and with God? What do you need to confess? What describes you that you wish didn't?

Just know this: Of all the lies we tell, the ones we tell ourselves are the deadliest. Unconfessed and unaddressed, they will continue to damage the people around us (and us) indefinitely. Level with yourself and with God. Everyone else knows your weakness. So does God. Why not admit it?

It's so easy to spot pride in others. But people who spot it in themselves and cultivate humility develop a much richer, much more fulfilling life.

PART VI

BURNOUT

11

LIKE FALLING OFF A CLIFF

How to Know When You're Burning Out

I t was 2006. My family and I had just landed back in Toronto after being at North Point Church in Alpharetta, Georgia, just north of Atlanta. You may have never heard of North Point Church, but I certainly had. Known for pioneering an amazing ministry, this church had been on my radar for a few years.

In 2005 I met Reggie Joiner, a brilliantly creative thinker and leader. We became fast friends, and he introduced me to his boss, Andy Stanley, who had become a hero to me over the years as I followed him from a thousand miles away. In my view (and the view of many others), Andy is one of the most gifted communicators and leaders of this generation.

Reggie invited me to speak at a conference at North Point in May 2006. At first, I thought he would want me to do a breakout session at the event, but he told me that, no, he had bigger plans. "Could you do a keynote?" he asked. If you know the church world even a *little* bit, you know that's like having the honor of playing in the Super Bowl.

I can still vividly replay in my mind the day I spoke—refining and revising my words endlessly, practicing the talk in front of my wife and kids for the hundredth time, ironing my shirt to perfection in the hotel room. I thought I was ready, but my nerves went a little ballistic when, during the sound check, the staff handed me my mic pack; it had "Andy" written on it.

I got introduced, and as I took the stage in front of twenty-five hundred leaders from around the world, I looked at the front row to see my wife and boys seated next to Reggie and Andy. Talk about intimidating.

So what happened? By most accounts the talk went well. Very well. The phrase *grand slam home run* was used more than a few times. More than a decade later, people still talk to me about that keynote. A few people referred to it as the talk of my life (which was a mixed-bag compliment—it's nice to peak at forty and have everything go downhill from there).

In many ways, I felt like I was at the top of the world. I had just spoken at one of the most influential churches in America, and apparently I'd done well. I was leading the fastest-growing and one of the largest churches in our denomination in Canada. Our ministry had attracted national attention, which apparently was expanding into international attention.

It doesn't get any better than that, does it?

Nothing prepared me for what happened next.

When the plane touched down in Toronto, I felt like I fell off a cliff.

Throughout my thirties, people told me that if I wasn't careful, I would burn out. I wasn't the best listener because I was, well, smarter than they were. Other (weaker) people might burn out, but I knew myself well enough and the work I was doing was important enough that it would never happen to me.

I thought I had come to the edge of burnout a few times, but I had seen the precipice each time and managed to pull myself back from it. I got some rest, took a vacation, scaled back my hours for a season, and—voilà!—problem solved.

I thought I could just do that forever. Until I couldn't.

That's the thing about burnout. Once you fall off the cliff, there's nothing to grab on to anymore. You're in free fall, and all the grasping and clamoring you do doesn't help a bit. For the first time in my life, I was hurtling headlong into the abyss.

BURNOUT IS . . . COMPLICATED

So what exactly happened to me in that summer of 2006? I still ask myself that question. Who really knows what corrodes the soul to the point where it disintegrates?

To be honest, this side of heaven, I'm not sure I'll ever be 100 percent certain of what happened. Burnout is complicated. But I do know this: in caring for others, I had not adequately cared for my own heart and soul or let others who wanted to care for me do so. I spiraled down for about three months before I hit bottom. I had been running hard for over a decade. Okay, maybe for three decades. Ambition tends to do that to you. I was the teenager who worked three jobs not because I had to but because I wanted to. I was the A student who completed three university degrees while holding down multiple jobs, getting married, and starting a family. I was the young pastor who didn't understand the word *no,* all the while thinking sleep and exercise were for people who had time for those things.

My accumulated fatigue played a big role, but burnout is deeper than that. In addition to the physical component, there were spiritual, relational, and emotional components as well. Those were the things I didn't pay much attention to until they ganged up on me and brought my life to a screeching halt.

Spiritually, I found myself in bizarre territory. I never lost my faith. I never stopped reading the Scriptures, and I still prayed. It's just that in the numbness that accompanied my burnout, I couldn't feel my faith anymore. I prayed, but it seemed like my prayers bounced off the ceiling. I read Scripture, but I no longer sensed that Scripture was reading me.

Relationally, it was strange. It felt like I had spent at least a decade with people taking small slices out of me. That's what leadership (and life) can be like sometimes if you're not careful. You know the feeling: it's like everyone just wants a piece of you—just a few minutes of your time, just a little advice, just a moment to look something over. And you give and give without replenishing, and eventually there's nothing left.

The emotional component of my burnout might have been the deepest. I had been going through counseling, and while in the long run it was tremendously helpful, in the interim it was deeply painful.

Over a period of years, I had come to realize that so much of my interior life was skewed. Thankfully, there was no headline—no affair, no stolen money, nothing that would attract anyone's attention. But there was an abundance of insecurity, jealousy, and fear and a deep misunderstanding of identity and fulfillment. I began to realize that at some point in my childhood, I'd concluded that love was earned by performance. The better I did, the more loved I would be.

That's not how love works at all, of course. But as a young, ambitious leader, I didn't know that. This distorted perspective led me into unhealthy cycles of performance addiction, a bad disease for a public speaker. I would finish a message on Sunday and ask my wife how it was. The exchange would always go something like this:

"What did you think of today's message, hon?"

"It was good."

"Good? As in, just *good*? You didn't think it was great?"

"Sure, it was really good. Great, I think."

"But really, do you mean that? Like how great?"

"Well, I think you helped a lot of people. It was a solid treatment of Scripture. Your delivery was strong."

"But was it, like, *really* great?"

Even as I type those words now, it looks like a conversation between an adult and a six-year-old, but then that's what happens with a lack of emotional maturity. The insecurity was deep enough that, as my wife pointed out on more than one occasion, no words were big enough or comprehensive enough to fill the void.

There would never be enough people, never enough thank-yous, never enough recognition to fill the hole deep inside. Apparently, it wasn't even enough to have my family, Reggie Joiner, and Andy Stanley in the front row raving about my talk, along with thousands of others. It doesn't matter how much water you pour in your bucket if your bucket is filled with holes.

A LONG, DARK SUMMER

All of that, and probably much more, went into my collapse that summer of 2006.

Within a month after I got off the plane in Toronto, my slide into the abyss was moving fast. My energy dropped to historic lows. So did my motivation and my mood. The drive that used to get me up early in the morning disappeared. And while I never stayed in bed all day, there were days when I felt I could.

My productivity tanked. Because most of what I do as a pastor is intellectual and relational, it's 100 percent dependent on the mental and spiritual energy I bring to my work. There was very little of either left. I found sermon writing difficult, connecting with people challenging, and even basic things like answering email next to impossible.

I started to develop a sort of anthropophobia (a fear of people) I'd never experienced before. I'm naturally wired as an extrovert. For most of my life, I had loved being with people, enjoyed working the crowd, and could often light up a room. That summer, I began to fear everyone.

I became deeply antisocial. I resisted going out and didn't want to talk to anyone other than my wife and kids. When we did go out—say, to be with our small group—I would park the car in the driveway and beg Toni to let me not go in. And when we did go in (usually), I would try to hide my six-foot-two frame behind my five-foot-three wife, hoping she would be my shield against humanity.

Perhaps the most disturbing part of my burnout was the loss of hope. I'm an optimistic person by nature, but that summer and for months afterward, hope was hard to come by. I lost hope that God could ever use me. I thought he was finished with my ministry and with me. I began to wonder if I could ever be of use to anybody, for work or otherwise.

A FALSE AND DEADLY FRIEND

My situation grew even darker than all that. Over a decade later, I still can't believe I'm going to write this next section. Part of me doesn't even want to admit this portion of the story is true. But it is, and I know this is an aspect of the experience far too many people can identify with.

By late summer, I began to think the best way to get through this burnout was to not go through it. Because hope had died for me in those months, I began to wonder whether that should be my preferred option as well. For the first time in my life, I began to seriously think that suicide was the best option. If I had lost hope, was no good to anyone, couldn't perform what I was expected to do, and was causing all kinds of pain to others (a conclusion that wasn't coming from a place of objectivity), then perhaps the best solution was to be no more.

By God's grace, I've never owned any weapons. If I did, I shudder to think about what I might have done to myself in a weak moment. I'm not terribly coordinated or technically skilled, so I figured a kitchen knife would probably result in me doing things horribly wrong. In my mind, my preferred path was to take my speeding car into a concrete bridge support and end things that way.

I don't know how close I came to doing it. I'm far from an expert at determining how serious a threat like that is. Although I never undid my seat belt and never sped up far past the limit as a bridge approached, I do know the thought of ending it that way became a false friend to me, a strange and perverse source of comfort. And, in a twisted way, maybe a way of getting back at a God and a life I felt were letting me down.

As I look back now, over a decade later, on how I felt at that time, it seems like it was someone else who struggled with those thoughts. It's amazing how an episode like this can play with your mind, but that's *exactly* what burnout does: it messes with your thinking. Its arena is your thought life, and burnout can be a merciless, savage beast. I'm so grateful I didn't listen to those voices, but I share this in case you might be hearing something similar. Do the people you love a favor: Don't listen. Don't give in. Don't give up. The negative voices are lying. That's not who you are, and that is definitely not the solution, even though some days it can feel like it is.

NOT JUST A FORTYSOMETHING ISSUE

A few years after my burnout ended, I nervously decided to talk to other leaders about it in the hope that it might help. The first time I delivered a talk about my burnout experience, in a similar way to how I prefaced my first talk on cynicism, I introduced it by saying, "If you're in your twenties or thirties, this talk may not mean a lot to you. In fact, you may want to just squirrel it away, and maybe someday it could help you or a friend of yours."

I wasn't ready for the mass of young adults who stood in line to talk to me after my presentation. Nearly all said, "I'm feeling so much of what you described too."

I had no idea. It's like burnout has become an epidemic. The more people I meet and the more I look around our culture, the more I think there may be many people suffering from burnout or what I might call "low-grade burnout." By that I mean the joy of life is gone, but the functions of life continue. You're not dead, but you're certainly not feeling fully alive. The symptoms are not enough to stop people in their tracks (like my burnout did to me), but they're present enough to sap the meaning and wonder out of everyday life.

SHOW ME A SIGN

More than a few of you reading this know you are on the edge of the cliff we call burnout. And probably a few of you are in free fall right now. What's so perplexing about burnout (and especially low-grade burnout) is that more than a few of the symptoms strike people as "normal." So how do you know if you're heading for burnout?

I'll describe eleven signs and symptoms I personally experienced as I burned out. If you recognize one or two of them, you're likely not burned out. Consider them warning signs. If you show six to eight, you may be in low-grade burnout or heading for the cliff. If you resonate with most or all of them, you're likely in full-fledged burnout. I hope these signs can help you see the edge before you career past it.

1. Your Passion Fades

Everybody struggles with lack of passion from time to time, but burnout moves you into a place of sustained motivation loss. Remember passion? It's what made you fall in love, stare at white clouds on a blue-sky day, jump up and down when you got accepted into your college of choice, and cry when you saw your firstborn. It's what infused your work with enthusiasm and made you a gifted, obsessive nerd at the hobby you used to pursue with a smile. Passion got you into all kinds of things, and it's one of the factors that makes both life and leadership wonderful over a long period of time.

When I burned out, my passion set like the sun. I knew what I was doing was important (leading a local church, raising a family), but I couldn't feel it anymore. I realized that a passionless person would never lead a passionate life. But I just couldn't find it anymore. My passion had died.

2. You No Longer Feel the Highs or Lows

If you're healthy, you *feel* things. You experience highs and lows. When I burned out, I couldn't feel either properly anymore. My main emotion was numbness. It was like my emotions had become a long drive through the Great Plains . . . flat for endless miles. If a friend had a baby, intellectually I knew it was an important moment that was supposed to generate joy, but I couldn't feel it. Conversely, if someone was sick or landed in trouble, I didn't really feel for that person either. I just felt numb.

Burnout numbs your heart, and this was one of the earliest signs for me that the edge was near. The numbing of my heart was something I had battled for three or four years before I fell headlong into burnout. Even now, I watch for it as a sign that something might be wrong.

You're designed to celebrate when people are celebrating and mourn when people are mourning.[1] If that's not happening, something's not right.

3. Little Things Make You Disproportionately Emotional

It's not that burned-out people feel zero emotion, but when you're burning out, you often experience inappropriate or disproportionate emotions.

Leading up to and during my burnout, little things started to set me off. Something like a missed deadline or a dishwasher that didn't get emptied might be a one or three out of ten on the problem scale, but I reacted like it was an eleven. That's never good.

Treating small things like big things and big things like small things are both signs that something deeper is wrong.

4. Everybody Drains You

People are a mixed bag for sure. Some energize you. Some don't. I get that. On this side of heaven, that's life. But when I burned out, *nobody* energized me anymore. Not even my family, my friends, or my leadership team. In my head, I knew they were good people, but my heart couldn't feel it. When nobody energizes you, they're not the problem. You are.

5. You're Becoming Cynical

We've already explored cynicism in chapters 1 and 2, but it deserves mention as a further sign of burnout. It's not that cynicism is itself proof you're burning out. You can be a cynic for a long time without burning out. But if you find your cynicism is advancing at a rapid rate, it may be a sign you're burning out. Cynicism never finds a home in a healthy heart.

6. Nothing Satisfies You

One of the hardest aspects of burnout was that nothing seemed to satisfy me anymore. Sleep didn't. Prayer didn't. Good people didn't. Recreation didn't. Vacation didn't. Work didn't. Food didn't. That's a sign of depression, and it's also a sign you're burned out.

7. You Can't Think Straight

When you're burning out, your heart messes with your head and you lose the ability to think clearly. I remembered having read enough about midlife crises and burnout to know that people make stupid decisions when they're burned out. So I had a daily conversation with myself that boiled down to five words: *Just don't do anything stupid.* This would include things like quitting my job or screaming at people. Some days, simply avoiding stupid is a win.

8. Your Productivity Is Dropping

One sign I knew indicated I was in burnout was my incredibly low productivity. I'm usually a fairly productive leader and person (some would say highly productive). But when I fell into burnout, even writing a simple email sometimes took an hour. My thoughts wouldn't come together. My pace slowed right down. And I felt like there was a cloud between me and everything I was trying to do. If you're working long hours but producing little of value, pay attention.

9. You're Self-Medicating

In the early stages of burnout, many people turn to self-medicating to numb the pain. This might involve overeating, overworking, sexual addictions, drinking, impulsive spending, or even drugs. When this occurs, you've chosen a path of self-medication instead of self-care to deal with the pain. I avoided drinking, drugs, and sex outside of my marriage. My medication was, ironically, more work, which just spiraled things downward. People who are burning out almost always choose self-medication over self-care.

10. You Don't Laugh Anymore

This seems like such a small thing, but it's actually a very big thing. If you're burning out, you don't laugh like you used to. I remember laughing out loud one day during my recovery after listening to something on the radio. It was then that it hit me: it had been months since I had laughed out loud. When you're burning out, nothing seems fun or funny, and at its worst you begin to resent people who enjoy life.

11. Sleep and Time Off No Longer Refuel You

If you're just tired, a good night's sleep or a week or two off will help most healthy people bounce back with fresh energy. If you're burning out, sleep and time off no longer do the trick. You could have a month off when you're burned out and not feel any difference. I took three weeks off during my summer of burnout, and I felt worse at the end than when I started. Not being refueled when you take time off is a major warning sign that you're burning out.

RECOGNIZE YOURSELF?

Some of you might be really alarmed right now because you're registering eight out of eleven symptoms—or maybe all eleven. Some of you might be concerned for your spouse or a best friend because you recognize the symptoms in him or her. So what do you do?

If you show any signs of burnout, I encourage you to seek immediate professional help. In my view, the best help will come from a combination of the care of a medical doctor and an excellent, trained Christian counselor. Your medical doctor will help you figure out how serious your symptoms are, and a skilled counselor will help you identify the reasons and conditions that caused you to burn out. If you're in a state of burnout or nearing it, I can guarantee that you have issues. I had a load of them. Toni had urged me to go to counseling for a few years before I actually went. I was too proud to go. I *sent* people to counseling, but I didn't want to *go* myself. How stupid. My wife saw issues I couldn't see. Others saw issues I couldn't see. And they were right. I was hurting others unintentionally.

The truth is that we all struggle with unresolved problems. And the sooner you deal with them, the better off you and everyone around you will be. Your unresolved past will sink your future unless you deal with it. That's what my unfinished business and unexamined issues did to me. They made me work insane hours at an unsustainable pace and see people as projects rather than relationships. I became a performance addict, and God needed to speak into that space so I could use the gifts he gave me in a healthy way.

Christian counselors helped me get to the bottom of that. I've seen a number of different counselors over the last fifteen years at different points, and each has played an instrumental role in my healing and spiritual formation. You may not need more than one, but for me, getting the right perspective at the right time has been so healing and freeing.

Why do I suggest a trained Christian counselor? First, not all counselors are great at what they do. Check for both credentials and references. Seek a recommendation from a trusted friend. Second, I am a firm believer in Christian counseling not just because I'm a Christian but because I believe the very heart of the problem of burnout is spiritual. If you leave Jesus out of the cure, you leave out much of the potential healing.

Speaking of healing, how do you move out of burnout? Believe it or not, you can come back. And come back more fully alive than you ever were before. That's what happened to me, and I'm not alone.

12

YOUR NEW NORMAL

Figuring Out How to Live Today So You Will Thrive Tomorrow

In the middle of my burnout, I wondered whether I would ever get better. I knew many in life had gone down this road before me, and what scared me is that some of them never made it back. Or even if they emerged from burnout, they were never the same again. Sometimes careers were done. Other times callings were abandoned. And sometimes, tragically, *they themselves* were done; hope never fully returned, and they didn't ever get back to being the people they were before.

That was the last thing I wanted to happen to me.

I was learning so much about myself, but diagnosis is different from cure. Knowing you have issues is different from the gentle and deep work of healing those issues. Every story is different, and the reasons for and depth of your burnout may be different from mine. As a result, your recovery may be different as well.

For me, I slowly began to recover with the love and assistance of an amazing wife, church board, leadership team, close friends, family, counselor, and a very gracious God. It took, honestly, a few years to really feel back at full stride again. I recovered 80 to 90 percent of my full strength in the first year. The last 10 percent took three or four more years.

Coming Back from Burnout

So how do you recover from burnout? Here are ten factors that helped me and many other people. We'll start there, and then we'll look at some principles that can help you avoid burning out (or burning out again).

1. Tell Someone

This was hard for me. It is for most leaders, especially guys. My guess is you will resist because of pride. And pride may be something that led you to burn out in the first place. Swallow your pride and tell someone safe that you have a problem. I know it's hard to do that, but as we've already seen, only humility will get you out of what pride got you into.

Whatever you do, don't keep your suspicions of burnout to yourself. Nothing good happens when you're isolated. The way through burnout is through community, even if you suspect that the impact of being in community was one of the factors that pushed you into burnout.

It's tough, but telling someone is the first step toward wellness. When you admit it to others, you also finally end up admitting it to yourself.

2. Develop a Circle Around You

Telling someone is different from seeking help. Your friends are a vital part of your recovery, but they don't have any training and are likely overwhelmed by the depth of your symptoms.

You wouldn't expect the buddy you go fishing with to treat your cancer, and similarly, he likely can't treat your burnout. That's why you need a doctor and a counselor. But your fishing buddy can walk with you through it.

And that's vital. You can't do this alone. Really, you can't. And often the simplest acts can make the biggest difference. One day a friend stopped by and simply said, "I know you can't feel it today, but the sun will rise again. It will." I can't tell you how much those words meant to me that day. Why do friendships matter? Because you need people who believe in you when you've stopped believing in yourself.

3. Keep Leaning into God

I know that, theologically, you might think this point should be first. After all, if God is real, isn't he also first? He is, for sure. And yet there are two challenges with this. First, if your emotions aren't working and you feel mostly numbness, you likely won't feel like God is there for you. But just because God seems silent doesn't mean he's absent. I did not feel God for months. Not when I prayed or read the Bible or worshipped.

Second, the more spiritual you are, the more you might be tempted to think that you and God can handle this privately. But God works through *people.* Sometimes the most tangible form of God's love is the love you receive from people who love God.

In my case, I never gave myself permission to quit my faith. I just kept reading Scripture, praying, and trusting, even on the bad days—especially on the darkest days when I felt least like trusting God. I'm so thankful I did. In pivotal moments like these, you will lean either away from God or into him. Lean in, hard. Even if you feel nothing. I did this, and eventually the feelings of intimacy returned. Just because you can't feel God's love doesn't mean he doesn't love you.

So don't give up. What I've learned is that obedience is greater than my emotions. Eventually your emotions catch up to your obedience. As you get healthier, your emotions begin to work the way they should. Sometimes they work better than they ever have.

4. Rest

I was so physically and emotionally tired when I burned out. Once burnout ground my pace to a halt, I realized just how exhausted I was. By July of my burnout summer, I understood how deep the problem was. I had talked to my board, had started seeking professional help, and was doing only as much as I could muster in my role as lead pastor of our church.

Once August came, I felt like I could no longer postpone dealing with my profound fatigue. Starting in early August, I slept for about ten hours a day for a month straight, adding naps on top of that. It took a month of intense rest for me to begin to come out of my numbness and feel some energy again. I had run so hard for so long, and the pace just wasn't sustainable.

It was then I began to realize that sleep is like money; deficits become debt, and debt needs to be paid off. I paid off my sleep debt that month, and I always try now to make sure I am not running a deficit. If I do for a week or two, I pay it off with more sleep. It shouldn't surprise any of us, even us type A personalities, that we were designed to spend about a third of our life sleeping and, on top of that, an additional one seventh of our lives resting. Now I guard my sleep zealously whether I'm at home or on the road. I almost never take red-eye flights because I'm a morning person and staying up late ruins my system for days. I've embraced naps. I've come to realize that most of us are like our phones. You start off in the morning with 100 percent charge, and at various points in the day, you need to be plugged back in. A quick nap at lunch can recharge me for a few hours. Getting seven to eight hours of sleep every night has become essential for me to perform at my best.

Someone once said that 70 percent of discipleship is a good night's sleep. That's about right in my view. If you're like me and most everyone else on the planet, you are at your kindest when you're most rested. So rest.

5. Find Something to Take Your Attention Away from Your Pain

The problem with pain is that when you slow down your pace, often you have only your pain to focus on. And pain is selfish; even emotional pain demands your attention. Not convinced pain is selfish? Drop a concrete brick on your toe and see if you can focus on anything else. At times, I found the emotional pain of burnout overwhelming. I knew if I kept focusing on the pain, it would occupy more and more space in my thought life and heart. I worried that the pain might paralyze me forever.

So what do you do? Distraction can be a powerful tool to get your mind thinking about other things. Watch a movie. Go out to dinner. Hit a hiking trail. Attend a party. It's not easy. One night we hosted a dinner party, and I left the table early and ended up crying in my bedroom for the rest of the night. But at least we threw the party. It got my mind off the constant cycle of depression. Eventually, not giving up on life helped me get back into life.

6. Do What You Can

You may need a long sabbatical, but sometimes you have to do the best you can to take care of yourself. I took off three weeks and then went back to work. When you're burned out, it's very easy to focus on what you feel you can't do, which some days feels like everything. I focused on doing what I *could* do, not on what I couldn't. In the years after my burnout, I talked to numerous friends who are medical doctors. They told me that doing what you can is a huge part of recovering from burnout. One physician said his instructions to patients can sometimes be as granular as "Today, I want you to brush your teeth." That sounds so simple, but when depression and exhaustion have a grip on your life, even brushing your teeth can seem impossible. The point? Keep moving. Do what you can.

I decided I'd preach once my three weeks of vacation were up. I had enough muscle memory to craft a sermon. The first weekend I preached (which was in August, the month of my exhaustion-debt repayment), those who knew my condition all told me, "We would have had no idea you were feeling so bad. You were amazing." I knew how I felt inside, but it was good to know I could still be helpful to others in some way.

What can you do today? Do it. Even if you don't feel like it.

7. Don't Make Any Big Decisions

As I shared earlier in this chapter, I was tempted to do more than a few things that could have ruined my life. I felt like abandoning my calling, running away from everyone and everything I knew, or driving my vehicle into a concrete wall. At some points, I created an alternate reality where I could stack boxes, wash cars, or cut grass for a living. Unlike my day job, at least in those lines of work I could see progress every day. It just seemed so much easier than what I was living through.

But I knew that one of the most important decisions I could make was to not make any big decisions, period. Over and over again, I told myself to not quit my job, have an affair, or buy a sports car. By the grace of God, I did none of the three. The first two will never be part of my long-term plan, but one day I would love to drive a '73 Corvette or new Audi.

Make your big decisions on a good day. And when you're burned out, you don't really have many good days. If you have to make a big decision (like changing jobs or relocating), lean into your circle of friends and people close to you who can help you prayerfully make a decision you won't regret.

8. Grieve Your Losses

A mentor of mine, Terry Wardle, once told me that ministry is a series of ungrieved losses.[1] He was right. The same is true of life. Life can be a series of ungrieved losses.

Think about how much loss is involved in life. Your best friend decides to move to another city. A much-loved uncle dies. You get passed over for a promotion at work. Your parents file for divorce after twenty-five years of marriage. Your car that was supposed to last another year gets towed away to the junkyard. Your spouse contracts a chronic illness. Many people pretend loss doesn't hurt when, in fact, it most certainly does. Worse than that, it's hard to know what to do with our losses. So we just go back to work and get on with life. For years when I read the scriptural stories of how people grieved, I thought, *What's wrong with these people? Why did they take forty days to grieve the death of Moses? Couldn't they just go to the funeral and head back to the office after lunch?* Little did I realize that taking the time to grieve your losses is one of the healthiest things you can do.

As I mentioned, I spent an inordinate amount of time sleeping in August 2006. I also spent an unusual amount of time that month crying. All the losses I ignored for decades couldn't stay inside anymore. To my utter shock, I just couldn't stop weeping. Eventually, the tears slowed. Then they stopped and fit into the normal pace and rhythm of life again. Once they left, I found closure, even healing. Now I pay much more attention to feelings of loss. I pray about them. I process them. Occasionally, I do shed tears over the deeper losses. And then I move on.

If you don't grieve your losses during your recovery, you're missing tremendous opportunities to put the past behind you. Otherwise, your past continues to sabotage your present and your future.

9. Reopen Your Heart

Because the symptoms of burnout include loss of passion, emotional numbness, and cynicism, chances are your heart has closed significantly during your burnout. It's vital that you reopen it.

As I mentioned in part 1, a contributing factor to my crash was broken trust in a few friendships. As hurt as I felt and as cynical as I was at points, I made a conscious decision to trust again and live with my heart open, not closed. It was a tough decision and an even harder process because an open heart leaves you vulnerable to being hurt and stung again.

But the wonderful thing is that so many people *are* trustworthy. Furthermore, God always is. And it means you will go on to have many new, deep friendships, rekindle and foster old ones, and actually experience the life you're living. Trusting again after your trust has been breached keeps your heart fresh and alive and—ultimately—hopeful again.

It's been over a decade since I burned out, and I still watch for the signs of burnout regularly. While that's important, living in avoidance mode isn't really living. It has to go deeper than that.

10. Live Today in a Way That Will Help You Thrive Tomorrow

If I've found an antidote to burnout, it's best summarized for me in a single sentence I developed as I worked through my recovery: *Live in a way today that will help you thrive tomorrow.* If I'm going to maintain wellness and avoid burnout again, I need to live in a way today that spiritually, emotionally, relationally, physically, and financially will help me thrive tomorrow.

Can you cheat for a day or two and let your attention to your well-being slide a bit? Of course you can. But I find if I cheat for a week or more, the cliff comes into view far more quickly than I'd like. And besides, what's the point of living your life in a way that simply avoids danger? Why would you not try to thrive rather than merely survive?

So how do I live in a way today that will help me thrive tomorrow? Maintaining health in all five major areas of life (spiritual, emotional, relational, physical, and financial) has become a top priority for me. Preburnout, I used to squeeze as much out of every hour and day as I could, and I thought health was a luxury I couldn't afford. You would think that taking the time to find health every day has *reduced* my effectiveness and productivity. Much to my surprise, both my effectiveness and productivity have multiplied. I've written four books in seven years, started blogging regularly, launched two podcasts, started speaking more widely, and had more time for my marriage, family, and friends. In addition to this, I'm in the best shape of my life. It's also multiplied my passion. I have more energy and enthusiasm for today and tomorrow in my fifties than I've ever had. The joy has never been deeper, and the opportunities have never been greater.

Nobody else is responsible for your health. You are. Pray, read your Bible, seek life-giving friendships, replenish your energy, eat right, work out, love deeply. These things nourish your soul. If you don't do them, nobody will.

A WORD TO ANY RESISTERS

When it comes to burnout, denial is an accelerator. Maybe you're thinking you're stronger than burnout. Chances are you're not. Remember, you've got control until you fall off the cliff. Then all control is gone.

Or maybe you think you're just tired or that the rules don't apply to you. Well, good luck with that. Every day you remain in denial, you make burnout *more* likely, not less likely. Rather than care for yourself and deal with your issues, you push on, closer to the edge than ever.

It's important to note that it's easier to find relief from the pace than from the weight. Pace can be controlled fairly easily. Take a day off. Shut off your phone. Cancel some meetings. Take a vacation. Put your feet up. Boom, your pace is adjusted.

But rest in and of itself will never bring you relief from the weight of life or leadership. The weight of life is heavy. Weight is what you *feel*. Weight is the tremendous responsibility many people find impossible to ignore, even when they're taking time off. Weight is the stress you feel over your marriage, kids, finances, growth, people issues, team dynamics at work, health, crises, and much more.

Pride and fear also play interesting roles when it comes to dealing with burnout. As we've already seen, pride will push you to think you can handle anything. Yet at some point you will come to the realization that you can't handle it. And at that point, pride's companion, fear, kicks in. And fear will keep you from telling anyone you can't handle it. Pride and fear are villains in the burnout story. They keep you first from admitting and then from telling. Both will tell you there's still too much of a stigma attached to burnout, anxiety, and even depression for many people to feel comfortable talking about them.

I hope this chapter is one more nail in the coffin of fear and pride. Admit this has hit home. Have someone who loves you read this chapter with you, go to the doctor with you, get you to a counselor, and pray for you if he or she will.

Breaking Bad

I *hated* my burnout. If you had talked to me in those first few months of my spiral, I would have told you I was convinced God had left me. Or was torturing me. If you've been in that space, you know what I'm talking about.

Hindsight is a gift. Instead, I now see God was doing something in the middle of my burnout. He was getting rid of parts of me that worked against myself, against him, and against others. And it hurt. He was opening new parts of my soul I had never seen. He was also forgiving me and helping me to forgive myself. He was helping me relate to people better. He was making me a better father, husband, leader, and friend.

This, again, is *sanctification,* the lifelong process of being made holy.

Holy can seem like a mystical term incapable of definition, but at its root it means "to be set apart." Sanctification is a process of going from what you used to be to being far more reflective of the character and nature of Christ. More humility, less pride. More love, less indifference. More kindness, less harshness. Whatever your faith perspective, most of us could agree that a person who is humble, loving, and kind will make a more positive contribution to this life than someone who is proud, indifferent, and abrasive.

We have an idea in our minds that God uses perfect people; that somehow we should all be humble, loving, and kind out of the box; and that if we are, God will use us. But if you dig a little deeper, that is categorically false. God's favorite people to use are the broken ones. Broken people have come to the end of themselves and learned there was not much there in the first place. Broken people get to the point that they realize the poverty within and have to look beyond themselves for renewal and strength. I believe God used me in life and leadership before he broke me during my burnout, but I also believe (and think others would concur) that now I am more responsive to God because there is less of me. That's what being broken does.

You'll be tempted to think God has left you in the dark night of your soul. But he hasn't. Like a surgeon, he's operating. And when you surrender to him, it works for your good and to his glory. This season in your life doesn't have to end in defeat. And when you surrender it to Christ, it doesn't, no matter how you feel.

GO DEEP AND L

A few years ago, a good f
and we spent time togeth

north of where I live. He leads a large church in the US and had slipped into burnout. Like so many others, he didn't see it coming.

Jeff had taken a thirty-day sabbatical and was determined to be back to 100 percent at the end of the month. He was at day fifteen of his sabbatical when we met, and his burning questions that day were "Carey, when will this be over?" and "How soon can I recover?" Then he added, "This is taking forever."

Those are the questions all of us A-types ask. I thought about the questions that day. I reflected on my own slow recovery and the work God did. We prayed together, and then I said to him, "Don't rush it and don't delay it. Let it take as long as it takes. Here's what I know, Jeff: if God wants to go deep, it's because he wants to take you far." The more I've thought about that insight, the more I see how true it is.

I would have gladly accepted a shallow brokenness for an immediate recovery. When your pain is deep, it's natural to think of any way to escape. Only now can I see how merciful, wise, and compassionate God was to take the breaking process as deep as he did. He knew what was ahead. I didn't. I still don't know all that's ahead, but God does.

There's also a promise underneath the pain. If God is doing surgery, it's because he wants to bring healing. It's a sign of his love. So let God go as deep as he wants to go. If he gets to the root of your disease, you will emerge a new creation. You'll still be you, but you'll be a different you, a more Christlike you.

One more thing happened on that visit with Jeff. As we walked down to the lake and he asked me questions about my burnout, I shared with him some of the things that I've shared with you in this chapter. And then a strange emotion hit me, an emotion I had never experienced before when thinking or talking about my burnout. I felt *gratitude,* actual gratitude that God was gracious enough to break me and lead me through it. It took nine full years for me to be able to feel thankful for what happened, but tears streamed down my face as we finished our walk.

Wherever this chapter finds you—maybe as someone who will never experience burnout because you can see it coming, as someone in the throes of low-grade burnout, as someone at the bottom of the pit, or as someone beginning to recover—I want you to know God isn't absent.

He's very present. In fact, if you will work with him, he'll do a great thing in your life. It bears repeating: if God wants to go deep, it's because he wants to take you far.

And because of that, perhaps one day you, too, will give thanks.

PART VII

EMPTINESS

WHEN ALL YOUR DREAMS COME TRUE

Why Money, Power, and Success Leave You Feeling Empty

know exactly how I felt on June 29, 2015. It's funny how you can relive the emotions of a particular day in detail. I can tell you what I was doing hour by hour, recalling the feelings that went with the events. In many ways, it was the day my internet dreams came true. Anyone who has ever created anything online (even a social media account) understands the daily tension of hoping a few more people might see what you posted. Even if you're not trying to build an audience or business online, we all know the sinking feeling when you post a picture of yourself doing something you love only to discover that three people like it.

If you understand that feeling, you understand the emotions of an on-line writer. I'm a goal-driven person, and the number of page views and visitors to my blog was a subject of fascination (okay, obsession).

On that single day in 2015, 436,000 people showed up on my blog in a twenty-four-hour period. In case you're wondering if that's normal traffic for someone like me, the answer is, um, no. In fact, that's not normal traffic for anybody whose name isn't Beyoncé or who isn't associated with the *New York Times*. For an average mortal like me, that's a crazy number of readers. It's equivalent to every single person in the city of Minneapolis or Tulsa ringing my doorbell to read what I'd written on a subject. Or to the Dallas Cowboys' stadium filling up 4.3 times to accommodate the crowd. Bananas. For the first time, I understood what the word *viral* meant.

It was a pretty exciting moment for sure. Any writer who tells you that it's all about self-expression and that readership doesn't matter is either lying or delusional. Of course you want people to read what you wrote; otherwise you wouldn't be a writer.

But this? I had never seen anything close to that. My previous *viral* piece garnered something like 24,000 views in a day, which alone was inconceivable for me. Yet on that summer day when some of the world showed up on my website, my eyes opened wider and my heart leaped higher every time I refreshed the stats page. By the end of the week, the post had reached over a million readers and had over a quarter million shares.

So how did that kind of success make me feel?

Surprisingly, the high didn't last nearly as long as I thought it might.

For starters, a million people didn't show up the next week when I posted fresh content. People got what they needed, and then they went back to their lives. Sure, my audience grew a bit and my regular readers were grateful as well, but the members of my momentary nation-state for the most part went their own ways.

Second, it created this sense that maybe I had peaked or that the traffic was a fluke. The likelihood of seeing that many readers again in a short window of time was small. Would I be happy writing for five or ten thousand people a day again? It was all so . . . anticlimactic.

Third, it made me wonder what kind of raging egomaniac I am. I have enough friends who blog to know that I'm not the only one who gets a rush out of numbers. Most of us check regularly, and as a general rule, most of us prefer more rather than less. Isn't that just human? But overall, the experience left me feeling far emptier than I thought it would, had someone told me that one day a bazillion people would read my blog. After a while, my response was a shoulder shrug. *Oh yeah, that many people actually did come one day.* It was a writer's dream come true. But the dream quickly left me feeling, well, empty.

RECOGNIZE THIS?

Not surprisingly, *empty* is a feeling I've had more than once in my life, most particularly after a peak. It happened after I graduated from law school, after our church became one of the largest in our denomination, and after we finished a few multimillion-dollar building projects.

Don't get me wrong. I'm grateful. Very grateful. And I realize some of this has been driven by insecurity, which I continue to work through. But feeling insecure ("I don't belong here; I don't deserve this") is a different sensation than simply feeling empty. Feeling empty is something I've seen afflict a surprising number of successful people. It's what causes lawyers making mountains of money to buy a lottery ticket and shout to their staff, "If I win this thing, you'll never see my face again."

In fact, the emptiness so many people experience in life is more intense in success than it is in failure. When you fail, you have nowhere to go but up. But when you're up, when you've done what others have only dreamed of doing and you still don't feel great . . . well, then what? Most of us have this notion that *Once I get to a certain place or achieve a certain thing, life will truly start in full, and I'll finally be happy and whole.* It just doesn't work out that way. You graduate, but you find there's still something inside you that says there has to be more. You find the one, get married, and have kids. And it's great, but still, what's that thing inside that says there must be more? You land a job and then a career job and then your dream position, but still, there's a quiet-but-real gnawing inside that says it's not all you imagined it would be. You pick different markers—time off, vacations, and savings goals—but still the high continues to be short lived. Keep going, and before you know it, you've convinced yourself retirement will fill the hole nothing else has been able to fill. It's quite the game.

It's also a game you lose. You've done everything you know to do, everything that was supposed to bring you satisfaction, and you still can't help but feel a bit empty. What gives?

THE RICHEST MAN ALIVE

At some point, most of us fantasize (even briefly) about what would happen if we had more money than we could ever spend, if we could just snap our fingers and whatever we desired would appear. Then we'd be happy, right?

Maybe you wouldn't feel as empty if you had so much money you never had to worry again. Or if you had your dream house, choice of exotic cars, and a personal chef to whip up magnificent omelets every morning and present dinner selections you can't even pronounce every evening. And, of course, in this scenario, you'd never sit in traffic again because your private helicopter or jet would whisk you away from it all.

We all have different ideas of what a great life would be, and maybe your ideal vision is more artistic, altruistic, or adventuresome. Maybe you'd quit your job, buy a vintage trailer, drive around the continent (or backpack around the world), and kiss mainstream culture goodbye. Just imagine for a moment that you could fill in the blanks to whatever your idea of paradise is: sleeping under the stars in Asia, extreme sports all the time, your best friend over all day every day, or even an endless summer on a white-sand beach surrounded by crystalline waters. Got the picture?

Regardless of what an idyllic life looks like to you, at any given point in every generation, somebody has to be the richest, most powerful human being alive. Three thousand years ago, it was a guy named Solomon. He didn't just hit the list for a day or two. He *was* the list. He had so much money that his personal surplus actually devalued silver for a generation.[1]

He was a Renaissance man before there was a Renaissance. He was a globally renowned expert on botany, history, philosophy, architecture, music, art, and astronomy. Solomon was Benjamin Franklin, Warren Buffett, and Albert Einstein stapled together. Throw Caligula in there too because he also had seven hundred wives and three hundred concubines (and you think *your* marriage is complicated).

If anyone had it all, Solomon did. World leaders came from around the globe to sit at his feet, and when they left, they said, "This was even better than the reports we heard." How often does that happen? Right, never. Except when Solomon was in the house. Toward the end of his life, he reflected on all of it. What he had to say is shocking. My *head* knows he's right, but my heart still screams, "No, he can't be! Give me the chance to prove him wrong. I'll take his money and influence, and I'll be happy. I will. I promise."

Solomon chronicled his rise to power, wealth, fame, and wisdom, as well as his attempt to find satisfaction in it all. He started out on an interesting foot:

Everything is meaningless . . . completely meaningless!
    What do people get for all their hard work under the sun?
Generations come and generations go, but the earth never changes.
The sun rises and the sun sets, then hurries around to rise again. The

wind blows south, and then turns north. Around and around it goes,
blowing in circles. Rivers run into the sea, but the sea is never full.
Then the water returns again to the rivers and flows out again to the
sea. Everything is wearisome beyond description.[2]

That's a fun way to start a conversation, isn't it? It's like Solomon's social skills had all disappeared in his old age or like maybe he should have
read about cynicism in part 1 of this book. But what he said is so valuable.
Through this passage, he walks us through the relentless climb to success,
which he scaled like nobody else, and tells us what the journey and destination were really like.

THE SMARTEST PERSON IN THE ROOM

Many people devote themselves to being as bright and clever as they can be,
either in their chosen fields or in life in general. I'm familiar with learning,
having three university degrees to my name (history, law, and theology). I
was not sprung into the full-time workforce as a contributing member of
society until I was thirty-one, so prolonged was my training. It's easy to
think the key to contentment is to *know* more. Take another course. Read
more books. Hang around brainy people. The thirst for knowledge can be
insatiable, and it can give you an edge. But does it satisfy the way you hoped
it would? Solomon was, by every account, brilliant. Here's what he found:

> I devoted myself to search for understanding and to explore by
> wisdom everything being done under heaven. . . .
>   I said to myself, "Look, I am wiser than any of the kings who
> ruled in Jerusalem before me. I have greater wisdom and knowledge
> than any of them." So I set out to learn everything from wisdom to

madness and folly. But I learned firsthand that pursuing all this is like chasing the wind.

> The greater my wisdom, the greater my grief.
> To increase knowledge only increases sorrow.[3]

Solomon found out firsthand that knowledge is both a blessing and a curse. Knowing more doesn't make you happier; in fact, he observed, it makes you sadder. This is true if you have a high IQ; it also becomes true as you gain knowledge of the human condition. The more you know about people, the more complex and challenging life becomes. After you buy a bike for your five-year-old, for example, you might realize that people steal kids' bikes, which makes you sad, both for your child and for the kind of people who do such a thing.

Solomon's knowledge made him smart, which also helped make him successful. He gained wealth, an esteemed reputation, and pretty much everything else this world has to offer. Remarkably, Solomon let us in on how he tried to use the trappings of power and influence to fill the void inside. He used much of his vast resources to self-medicate the haunting emptiness he felt amid his success. It's a pattern I've seen repeated again and again in people, especially successful people. You don't have to be the richest man alive to understand the struggle. Monday through Friday not doing it for you? Well, there are other options. Solomon explored them to the fullest extent.

PARTY ON, MY WAYWARD SON

Frustrated by the lack of fulfillment that knowledge and power brought him, Solomon decided that fun seemed like a decent option. Frankly, fun is an option many people turn to. About 70 percent of the US workforce is disengaged at their job—hate it actually.[4] And what do you do when you hate your job? If you're like most people, you live for the weekend.

Solomon tried that too. His weekends seemed pretty awesome. He wasn't exactly at a borrowed lake house riding a twenty-five-year-old teal Jet Ski that runs only when you reattach the battery cable properly, like many of us. If you've got the money, you make the fun come to you. Which he did. You bring some friends over, laugh, relax, pretend every night is Friday night, and alter your mind a little bit, right? Solomon's been there:

> I said to myself, "Come on, let's try pleasure. Let's look for the 'good things' in life." But I found that this, too, was meaningless. So I said, "Laughter is silly. What good does it do to seek pleasure?" After much thought, I decided to cheer myself with wine. And while still seeking wisdom, I clutched at foolishness. In this way, I tried to experience the only happiness most people find during their brief life in this world.[5]

Partying is a great way to self-medicate. It effectively masks the dull ache. Gather some friends, crank the tunes, crack open a bottle, light up whatever you're lighting up, and soon you forget your troubles. I'm not saying this is good; I'm just saying it happens millions of times every weekend because people don't know what else to do.

Solomon got that. Did you catch that last part of what he said? Don't miss it. He said the *only happiness* a lot of people experience in this life is a buzz on the weekend. Partying is a telltale sign there's something missing in your life. In fact, most people who party hard don't know why they do it. Sometimes the self-medicating emerges before the diagnosis. If your one glass of wine has become three (or the bottle), you're playing pharmacist with prescriptions that are no longer being taken as directed, or you're hoping your state soon legalizes what you're enjoying, it's a clear sign that you're self-medicating some deeper angst.

Solomon saw the pain first and applied the party Band-Aid later. But many people party first and only later discover what the pain is. Sometimes, they never discover what got them there in the first place. It's like Jack Nicholson was paraphrasing Solomon when he asked, "Is this as good as it gets?" Too many people have concluded that getting drunk or high *is* about as good as it gets in this life. I guess if everything else leaves you feeling empty, at least you don't notice it for a few hours. Solomon partied for a while but checked out of the scene over time, concluding it was also meaningless. He moved on to other things.

HAVE YOU SEEN MY CAR COLLECTION?

Partying isn't the only way to escape emptiness. Retail therapy is another well-established way to self-medicate. Successful people find themselves with the ability to buy and accumulate a lot in their lives, and Solomon had more money than he could spend. But he decided to try anyway.

And that leads us into a fascinating journey. A long time ago, someone shared with me a progression to success and accumulation. It's simple but way too true. Almost all of us engage in it in some form, and the more money we have, the truer it is.

Ready? Once you understand it, you'll see it everywhere:

- More
- Better
- Different

That's the progression. You start with *more,* move to *better,* and end up at *different.* Let me explain.

The first thing you do when you start making enough cash to move beyond just paying the mortgage and buying groceries is accumulate more. Your four-cylinder gas miser becomes your second car, and you add an SUV for the family (most urbanites drive SUVs because you never know when you might encounter a gravel driveway). You get out of your starter home and into bigger square footage. Your wardrobe expands. So does your pantry because now you can afford two bags of Cheetos (which may also explain why your wardrobe is expanding). The first step into success is *more*.

But soon you notice everyone has a little more, and you wonder how to differentiate yourself. So you move from *more* to *better*. You kiss your domestic SUV goodbye for some German engineering. Your bigger home gives way to a custom home. You upgrade to a better TV with a nice home theater system. You trade the extra Cheetos for organic Cheetos. (At your upscale health-food store, they're called "Artisanal, Hand-Crafted, Naturally Sourced Cheese Puffs." That's gotta be worth eight dollars right there.) You have traded *more* for *better*. But it's still not quite enough because your friends also have better things now too.

The final rung on the ladder is *different*. Others may have more and better, but this is unique, special, and rare. You can't just join this golf club; you have to be invited. They always give you this table at this restaurant, but you know the wait list is three months long. Yes, this is an early copy of *The Hobbit*, a true first edition actually. It's from the original printing of just fifteen hundred copies in September 1937. Oh, and have you seen my car collection?

If you do *different* well, everything in your life is scarce or custom. Even your dog has a bespoke doghouse. (Did you know Barfy's house was crafted with rare Brazilian walnut inlays?)

Climb high enough on the success ladder, and *more* will bring you to *better. Better* will drive you to *different.* Where does *different* take you? According to Solomon, who could do *different* better than anyone alive, it takes you to *despair.* Here's his take on *more, better,* and *different:*

> I also tried to find meaning by building huge homes for myself and by planting beautiful vineyards. I made gardens and parks, filling them with all kinds of fruit trees. I built reservoirs to collect the water to irrigate my many flourishing groves. I bought slaves, both men and women, and others were born into my household. I also owned large herds and flocks, more than any of the kings who had lived in Jerusalem before me. I collected great sums of silver and gold, the treasure of many kings and provinces. I hired wonderful singers, both men and women, and had many beautiful concubines. I had everything a man could desire!
>
> So I became greater than all who had lived in Jerusalem before me, and my wisdom never failed me. Anything I wanted, I would take. I denied myself no pleasure. I even found great pleasure in hard work, a reward for all my labors. But as I looked at everything I had worked so hard to accomplish, it was all so meaningless—like chasing the wind. There was nothing really worthwhile anywhere.[6]

That's a fairly universal indictment of the ladder of success. And it's not just the emptiness of *things.* Your climb from junior associate to the C-suite was fast and celebrated, but still, all that advancement and all that success leave you feeling vacuous. The strange part, of course, is that what was supposed to bring you satisfaction doesn't. It's not that you're ungrateful. In fact, your success and the emptiness that accompanies it make you feel guilty. You *are* grateful, and you realize that you have it much better than so many others, but the lingering question remains: *Really, this is it?* That combination—"I know I should be thankful and I am, but really?"—engenders a deep and profound angst.

You know you should be happier than you are. So why do you still feel empty? Why didn't any of this do what you thought it would do? Why is there a gnawing hollowness underneath it? Solomon could empathize, and I'm going to suggest his net worth and climb to the top outpace yours by a wide margin. He got to the very top. And it was empty.

THE CYCLE IS CRUEL

Tragically, what many people turn to for reconstruction ends up bringing more destruction. The solutions we chase just end up introducing more problems. Just as you can spend hundreds of thousands of dollars and decades of your life chasing *more, better,* and *different* only to come up short, people try to numb the pain of emptiness with things that make the hollow worse, not better. There are far more false comforters than real comforters in this area. I'll run us through two more options before we get to the antidote, not to depress you, but to identify what we *think* will help, though they rarely do.

1. More Work

If you're someone who's not into the party scene because you don't want to mess up your life with substances, trivial pursuits, or other distractions, you still have to deal with emptiness. It's easy and even natural to throw yourself harder into your work or to start a side hustle to consume your time.

This was an easy trap for me to fall into. Since I'm a Christian and a pastor, drugs or drinking too much alcohol were never really options of escape for me, but work, well, that was different. Workaholism is the most rewarded addiction in America today. You may get fired for drinking too much, but working too much usually gets you promoted. It will also get you a raise.

When I look back on my first decade in leadership, I realize that my crazy hours at work were masking the emptiness I felt when I stopped. One of my greatest fears as a man in my thirties was, as Pascal suggested, being alone with my thoughts. I loved the rush of being busy, being needed, and seeing progress at our church. When I was home, I wanted people around and constant activity. When I was alone, I always wanted something to do. I even made sure I had music on all the time. Being alone and quiet made me deeply uncomfortable and soon revealed the emptiness inside. It's ironic how the quiet on the outside can reveal so much disquiet on the inside.

For me, the hours I put in at work were a significant contributing factor to my burnout (as I described in part 6). But at the time, running hard into the future was an easy way to run from the emptiness. Until, of course, I hit a wall.

If you're working too many hours, do you know why? You might say, "Oh, it's just a busy season." But don't fool yourself. I used to say that all the time. You know what's true about seasons? They have beginnings and endings. If your season doesn't have a beginning and ending, it's not a season; it's your life. Remember, working is healthy; overworking is not.

2. All You Can Eat

Overeating is another crippling form of self-medication our culture has embraced wholeheartedly. And when I use the word *crippling*, it's not in the metaphorical sense. Globally, obesity now kills three times more people than malnutrition does.[7] And even if it doesn't kill you, it can significantly affect the quality of your life. Being overweight or even obese is almost normal in many circles today in Western culture.

As someone who has to watch my weight very carefully (usually I watch it go up), I empathize. I love food, and I love to eat far more than I love to exercise. The challenge is that overeating is relatively socially acceptable. Just like workaholism gets you promoted, overeating gets celebrated. When was the last time you were at a dinner party and the host served you bean sprouts and tofu and told you to eat less than you had on your plate? Right, never.

No, we celebrate the company of others by indulging. I do it too. Gourmet dishes, tantalizing barbecue, and dessert—never forget dessert. We even do this in church. The potluck dinner is too often just a socialized and sanctioned form of gluttony. Food is the drug of choice for many Christians. At its heart, overeating is the same old problem Solomon wrote about, just in a different form. Being full doesn't cure emptiness either.

APPETITE FOR SEDUCTION

So what fuels the cycle of self-medication and the insatiable desire for more? Underneath the constant pursuit of more (more work, booze, pills, food, sex, or things) is an *appetite*. And appetites are strange things.

Think about it. Your appetite makes you discontent with what you have. Then it convinces you that what's next will satisfy it. It seduces you into believing that what you know isn't true ("I've never been satisfied before") is true ("But I will be satisfied next time"). Solomon phrased the tension so well: "No matter how much we see, we are never satisfied. No matter how much we hear, we are not content."[8] As we've already seen, food is a classic example of this dynamic. Whether you tend to overeat or not, when something tastes amazing, your immediate reaction is to simply want more, thinking it will satisfy your appetite.

Some people stop, but most of us don't, and then we fall into an appetite-induced downward spiral. The reality, of course, is that eating more makes you crave more. If you do this enough times, your stomach will physically expand to accommodate more food and you will become an overeater. At that point, you're eating far more than you used to, and *still* your cravings are never satisfied. That's a powerfully destructive combination. That's what every form of self-medication does to you: it makes you crave more.

The challenge with more is there's no finish line. There's no end. How much work is enough? How many promotions? How much food, sex, money, or power will it take? How many pills? How much alcohol? If your answer is simply more, you need a better answer.

SELF-MEDICATION OR SELF-CARE?

If you're self-medicating, what should you do? Obviously, if you've developed an addiction, the best thing you can do is get help. Go see your doctor and check yourself into rehab. Do what it takes to break the incessant tug of addiction. Counseling is a great idea as well. If you don't know what's driving your addiction, you'll get driven back to it again and again.

But once you've kicked an addiction, what do you do then? That's where self-care comes in. We've covered many aspects of self-care elsewhere in this book, but let's cover a few more. I've personally found that anytime I start to self-medicate (and my two usual poisons are more work and more food), the best immediate remedy is self-care. Think about it: when you're self-medicating, you're probably ignoring some of the fundamentals you shouldn't neglect. As we've seen already in this book, self-care is a vital component of true life. The emptiness of life will push you to self-medication, and when you end up there, the quickest path out is self-care. It's also a way to keep you out of the ditch in the first place, as people who practice self-care rarely self-medicate.

To truly care for yourself, come back to this question daily: What do I need to do (or not do) so I can live today in a way that will help me thrive tomorrow? That question will serve as a filter that will push you to rest when you're tired, stop eating when you're full, work out when you need to, put the brakes on your appetite, renew your heart, and do whatever else you need to do to thrive.

Self-care might stop the insanity of self-medication, but it can't solve the basic human condition of emptiness. So what does? I'll share with you the only thing I know that can do it.

MY KINGDOM COME?

Getting over Yourself
Isn't as Scary as You Think

Everyone has a backup career. You know, that thing you'll do with your life if your current job vaporizes or you quit one day in a rage? You probably have one. I have dozens of them, and since rock star seems out of reach at this point, sometimes I think about marketing. If everything fell apart, maybe I could work at a creative firm trying to get disinterested people interested in new things.

Because of this interest, I've paid attention to marketing theory and trends over the years, and one of the principles of Marketing 101 is understanding what marketers call WIFM: "What's in it for me?" (They pronounce it "whiffim.") Every good marketer knows that if a product is ever going to sell, the marketer has to answer the WIFM question well.

You intuitively understand this. The only reason you as a consumer will ever buy a product (whether it's laundry detergent or a new laptop) is because you believe it will make your life better. You believe the answer to WIFM is that the value of the product matches or exceeds its price point. If something you purchase doesn't make your life better or brings you less value than what you paid for it, you'll want to return it. If you can't do that, you'll vow to never buy it again.

To accelerate WIFM, advertising also takes you on a strange journey. As we saw earlier, marketers create discontent with what you have. Your current shirt (or phone, fridge, or car) isn't good enough anymore. It's too old, too slow, too faded, or too clunky, and as a result you need a new one that's faster, brighter, sleeker, and better. So you buy a new one, and all your problems are solved. Until next year. Then, manufacturers introduce a *better* version to the market, and what you just bought is now too old, too slow, too faded, or too clunky. And so the cycle repeats itself.

Guess how that leaves you feeling? Perpetually discontent. And if you're not careful, it also leaves you broke. Nothing's ever good enough for long. And the discontent makes you feel empty. You've run everything through a "you" filter your entire life, and you're still not happy.

Worse, because the WIFM formula has so permeated culture, you take that mentality into everything you do. Think about marriage. The secret question we all ask in relationship to our spouse is "What's in it for me?" That question can infect your parenting, which is why you're not just upset at your kids when they mess up but also upset about how it reflects on you in front of your family and friends. Your kids are not delivering the stream of constant joy you had hoped they would bring you. And if they are, then it makes you feel great in front of your family and friends, which lands you right back into the jaws of pride.

Sigh.

There is no end to the sad discontent of making *you* the mission of your life. No job has quite delivered what you hoped for. Maybe it did for a while, but not for long. Even your friendships can get old fast because, well, what have they done for you lately? If WIFM becomes your spiritual filter, watch out. No church will be good enough, no group will be good enough, and God will seem only as good as he's been to you lately. It all leaves you feeling so empty, so disillusioned, and so sad. (Okay, maybe I'd make a terrible marketer, come to think of it. This chapter is basically premature career suicide.)

All of this, however, leads us to the antidote to emptiness. In many ways, the antidote is a giant nail in the coffin of WIFM.

Ready? If you want to beat emptiness, *find a mission that's bigger than you.* As long as you keep making your life all about you, you'll experience one round of emptiness after another. Like most worthwhile things in life, that idea is easy to understand and very difficult to live out. What exactly does it mean to have a mission in life that's bigger than you? By default, virtually everything inside you will work against a mission that's bigger than you. The wheels are already turning. *If I don't look out for me,* you're thinking, *who will?*

It's even deeper than that. You are someone you've woken up with every single day of your life. You are the common denominator in every experience you've ever had. As a result, you filter all your experiences, all your learning, all your relationships, and everything that's come to you in this life through your own eyes.

This is exactly why you need to stop making *you* your mission. You need a mission that's far bigger than you. Even if you "found yourself" in that postcollege trip a few years ago, now you need something bigger than that. So how does your need for a mission that's bigger than you play itself out? When you look for it, you'll see it everywhere you turn.

NOBODY REALLY WANTS TO WORK FOR YOU

One of the reasons 70 percent of employees are disengaged at work is because people don't understand the greater purpose or mission behind what they do, and most managers and leaders never try to move people toward something greater. If a worker's mission is about himself, and a manager's mission is about herself, it's pretty easy to see the clash coming.

A number of years ago, a thought gripped me: *Nobody really wants to work for me.* What I mean by that is not that nobody wants to work for *me.* I've been fortunate to have some great teams, many of whom I've worked with for years. But even as a senior leader in an organization, I've realized the ultimate motivation isn't that people want to work for *me.* Serving me isn't much of a calling. Neither is serving you. You know what motivates people to engage deeply at work? A mission that's bigger than you and me—a cause that gets them out of bed in the morning. They want to make a difference. People want to make the world a better place. They want to put a dent in the universe. And if I as a leader can help them do *that,* I'll have a motivated team for years to come.

Whether you just launched a start-up, supervise a shift at a coffee shop, manage a large division, or are the CEO of a Fortune 500 company, if padding your paycheck is the main objective for your employees, they'll quit. If their forty-plus hours are just about lowering costs, raising the bottom line, and ensuring a great third-quarter earnings report to shareholders, they're going to ultimately disengage.

Money isn't the mission. Money *funds* the mission.

You aren't the mission. Your job is to point people to the mission—a mission worth spending a major chunk of their lives working toward.

Give people a cause, a mission to make a difference in the world, a way to help others, and they will rally. Let them know their efforts have made a difference in someone else's life, and they'll look forward to getting themselves out of bed.

Almost every company gets started because the founders want to solve a problem, whether that's unclogging people's drains at a fair price, brewing a better cup of coffee in a chic atmosphere, or putting a person on Mars. There's a cause that's bigger than just working for the boss or turning a profit. It calls out the best in us, moves us to do something bigger. But along the way, we forget that this is what motivates people.

MY KINGDOM COME

Why is it that mission motivates in a way that *me* never does? Why is it that trying to satisfy our needs is so unsatisfying in the end? I believe it has to do with the very purpose of life. About a thousand years after Solomon wrote down his observations about the futility of it all, Jesus got to the essence of the frustration we all feel and proposed a rather radical solution: "If you try to hang on to your life, you will lose it. But if you give up your life for my sake, you will save it."[1] In other words, the very thing we fear most—surrendering control of our lives—is the key to life.

In the process of trying to find life—to claim it as our own and to build, acquire, accumulate, succeed, find, and create in the hope of finding deep satisfaction—we lose it if the goal is self-fulfillment. But in the very act of surrender, of giving up our lives, we find life. Jesus's words have meaning on more than a few levels. First, this is clearly an invitation to trust your life to him as Savior. It's his invitation to make him the savior and leader of your life. In my view, that's the most important decision you can make in your life. The real you is found only in a life-giving relationship with Christ.

But Jesus's words move beyond that. If we simply trust him and become Christians, you and I will quickly slide back into the Kingdom of Me. Our relationship with Christ and our approach to life will be about what we can get out of it all: *What's God done for me lately? What's Christ going to give me next?* It's so easy to love the gift more than we love the giver and to turn our lives into quests for happiness, with God as one more weapon in our arsenal. It explains why so many Christians grow disillusioned and walk away. God as a vending machine is bad theology, especially when you drop your dollar in and the candy bar doesn't come out.

It also explains why so many people who wouldn't consider themselves Christians get frustrated with the self-centeredness of Christians who are clearly pursuing their own selfish interests. Maybe they're going to heaven, but they're going to try to take as much from this earth and from others as they can while they're here. They haven't surrendered to a bigger mission. They're not living for a cause that's bigger than they are.

Wherever you find yourself spiritually, ask yourself this question: *Which kingdom am I living for?* Left unchecked, I will always live for the Kingdom of Me. Even as a Christian, I can let my prayer life and my overall life quickly become "My kingdom come; my will be done." If you're not sure about this, just hang out at a Christian prayer meeting for a while. The requests are often a long list of everything we want God to do. It's as though we need to inform, advise, and correct God because, clearly, he needs more information. We're not sure we can trust him, so our list is long.

God does indeed want us to express what we need or even what we want. But telling him these things shouldn't be at the heart of the relationship. Prayer is not a button to be pushed; it's a relationship to be pursued.

If I pray for my will to be done, I get more of me. If I pray beyond that—if I pray for God's will to be done—I get more of God. In all honesty, whose kingdom are you pursuing?

A Terrifying Alternative (but You Already Know This)

The alternative to living for yourself is dying to yourself. I realize how terrifying that sounds. It's appalling to me too.

But if you think about it more deeply, you'll instantly realize that it's a pretty good deal. Which is why I keep surrendering to it. After all, the people you admire the most are never *selfish* people. Selfishness looks good only to the selfish in the same way that pride is attractive only to the proud. Humility will win you what pride never will: the affection of others. And that's exactly what selflessness will do. Other people naturally gravitate toward people who live for a cause beyond themselves.

If you think through to the logical conclusion, the only thing more terrifying than dying to yourself is living for yourself. Remember where a life devoted to self ultimately leaves you? Right. It leaves you alone. The most selfish people you know drive others away from themselves. Selfishness breaks up marriages, destroys relationships between parents and children, ruins friendships, and in the workplace makes you a leader no one wants to follow. And all along, you'll wallow in self-pity wondering why no one likes you.

Conversely, when you die to yourself, something greater rises. When you are no longer all about you—when you are over yourself and live beyond yourself—you're finally in a position for God to use you and for others to see the joy in being with you.

Flip back to the funeral scene we imagined in chapter 3 (the one where your family reduces your entire life to a few paragraphs and eventually a single sentence). You know what families remember? "Oh, he was selfless in his devotion to Mom." Or "She gave up so much to make sure we had what we needed." Similarly, your employees will remember you not because you produced outstanding quarterly results but because you were kind to them. You cared about them. You helped them. You called out the best in them as you pursued something bigger than all of you put together.

The Kingdom of Me is a sad kingdom. And one that leaves you feeling so empty.

Die to it.

A Life That's Bigger Than You

To be honest, as a church leader I've always felt like I've had an unfair advantage when it comes to finding a mission bigger than me. That's because I'm convinced the church has the best mission in the world. Regardless of how you phrase it, the church's mission usually comes down to helping people move into a growing relationship with Jesus Christ. For most of my adult life, I've had the privilege to invest myself in that mission and help others do the same.

What about you? How do you find a mission that's not about you? I encourage you to put Christ at the center of your mission. Maybe you already do that, or maybe you're not quite there yet. I know this for sure: the emptiness inside you will go away only when you decide to stop making life all about you. You need a mission bigger than you.

Whatever that is, when you die to yourself, something far greater will emerge. The silence won't be haunting anymore; it will be exciting. You'll have time to reflect, pray, dream, and imagine a better world.

Your interactions with people will improve greatly as you begin to think about what you can give rather than what you can get. Self-care will become far more attractive than self-medication. The possessions you have will be less about using them for personal enjoyment and more about using them to help others. And even your accomplishments will be far more closely tied to fulfilling a mission than they used to be.

And in the process of giving your life away, you'll find it.

Conclusion

CALVIN MEETS HOBBES

S o maybe there *is* an alternative to Thomas Hobbes's previously mentioned observation that life is nasty, brutish, and short. I hope this book has pointed you in that direction. But how do you tie all this together? How do you make sure you *can* see it coming if emptiness, disconnection, cynicism, or anything else we've touched on is headed your way? How do you keep Hobbes's observation from becoming your epitaph?

Years ago, as another lawyer, John Calvin, was trying to figure out the meaning of life, he began his treatise on Christianity and religion with this line: "Without knowledge of self there is no knowledge of God."[1] It's fascinating that a man known for his theology (his thinking would later be called Calvinism) began with *self*-knowledge. Calvin believed that those who don't know themselves will never fully know God.

That's a challenge for those of us who call ourselves Christians. Sometimes Christians can overspiritualize life. It's so much easier to look upward or outward than it is to look inward. To look inward—to hold our lives up to a mirror—exposes the depth of our failings, and frankly, most of us would rather focus on the failings of others. But Calvin started there. He said if you ever hope to know God, you need to know yourself.

Let me ask you a question: How well do you know yourself? Truly?

Sure, I would think as you've now read through this book, you might answer by saying, "Well, better than I used to." And that's a great start. But the point Calvin was making runs deep. Self-knowledge will take you into profoundly meaningful places. Socrates put it another way: "The unexamined life is not worth living." (Who knew Socrates and Calvin would be friends?)

So what will help you see it coming every time? Even in subjects this book doesn't cover and with issues you've never even thought about? Simply put, self-awareness coupled with a close walk with God will. When you are intimately in touch with your own emotions and inclinations and deeply knowledgeable about the ways of God, you'll have a much greater chance of seeing it—whatever *it* is. Self-aware people have a conscious knowledge of their motives, desires, feelings, and character. They are also in tune with how their actions affect others. The more self-aware you are, the more likely you are to see it coming.

Years ago, Daniel Goleman shook the world with a new theory: that emotional intelligence was as or even more important to success than intellectual intelligence.[2] He argued that this is true in life and in leadership. His theory on emotional intelligence has shaken up the business world (and arguably *the* world). Goleman identified five main components for emotional intelligence, chief of which is self-awareness. In fact, if you grow in self-awareness, the other four factors of emotional intelligence (self-regulation, motivation, empathy, and social skills) become so much easier to master.

What Self-Aware People Know That Others Don't

The question, then, becomes, How well do you know yourself? One way to test your level of self-awareness is to figure out what self-aware people know that others don't. In my experience, there are four things. They seem straightforward enough, but it's surprising how many people live day to day unaware of them.

1. Their Impact on Others

Of all the characteristics of self-aware people, this is the most endearing. Self-aware people understand not only what their own emotions and actions are but also how their emotions and actions affect others. Think about disconnection. The key problem I had is that I didn't realize what it was like to be on the other side of me.[3]

That sounds simple, but the implications are staggering. Think about it. How many times have you had a bad day only to not know *why* you're having a bad day? And then how many times has your mysteriously bad day had a negative impact on your spouse, your kids, and your coworkers? Far too often, right? Me too. That's what self-awareness and emotional intelligence start to address in us. They stop that. Self-aware people refuse to let a bad day on the inside spill out to others on the outside. And even when they do allow this to happen, they realize they're hurting others and apologize or take other steps to mitigate the damage.

When you stop using *your* emotions as the only filter through which you process your attitude and actions, you grow as a person. You self-regulate and become more interested in other people than you are in yourself. If you want to become more emotionally intelligent, be aware of the impact your emotions have on others.

2. Their Weaknesses

Nobody likes to admit he or she has weaknesses, but we all have them. The longer I live, the more I realize how small my sweet spot really is. I do only a few things well, and for everything else, it's downhill from there. Your understanding of and respect for your weaknesses actually make you easier to work with and more valuable to the people around you. We've all met the person who wants to sing in the band but can't carry a tune. Self-aware people understand their weaknesses and limit their activities in areas where they are not gifted. This does two things:

- It creates space for others to shine.
- It allows them to spend most of their time working from their strengths.

Think about the impact that admitting your weaknesses might have on your family alone. Then take that into the workplace. It takes real humility for people to admit where they are not strong, but that characteristic is so endearing.

3. Their Strengths

While it may take humility to acknowledge your weaknesses, acknowledging your strengths doesn't mean you're proud. You have gifts, skills, talents, and abilities, and it's selfish not to lean into them. If you use your gifts as part of a larger mission and for the benefit of others, you'll actually avoid the emptiness so many people feel otherwise.

There's also evidence that people who don't operate out of their gifting are more vulnerable to crashing in life and leadership. Top leaders who have affairs or embezzle money are often leaders who were operating in a position that wasn't requiring them to fully lean into their strengths.[4] If you regularly do what you were created to do, the likelihood of growing cynical, disconnected, proud, or irrelevant diminishes.

And what about that humility thing again? Well, self-aware people know what they're best at but don't brag about it. They just do it.

4. Their Limits

One of the deadliest mistakes you can make is to ignore your limits. Ignoring my limits was a significant factor in pushing me into burnout. As much as you may push back on your limits, they're still there. Self-aware people have a realistic sense of what they can do and what they can't do, where they end and where others need to begin. When they need a break, they take one. When they're tired, they acknowledge it and take responsibility for getting some rest. When they're running on all cylinders, they give whatever they've got to whatever they do.

Again, everyone benefits: their coworkers, their friends, and even their family.

Ironically, leaders who know their limits often operate much closer to their potential than leaders who have no idea where their limits are. Knowing your limits, rather than being unaware of them, makes you far more effective.

WHERE DOES SELF-AWARENESS TAKE YOU?

Deep self-awareness, Calvin argued, eventually pushes us away from ourselves and back toward God because it makes us "displeased with ourselves."[5] Calvin was convinced that the more deeply we look inside, the more despairing we might become.

When I was burning out, I dug more deeply into the depths of my heart and soul than I ever had in my life. I came to the sobering realization that there wasn't nearly as much good in my soul as I thought. I saw an intense futility that bothered me, and I became more aware than ever before of my powerlessness to effect change in my life.

Calvin said this is exactly what drives us back to God. I gave you only half of his equation earlier, so let me share the rest: "Without knowledge of self there is no knowledge of God. . . . Without knowledge of God there is no knowledge of self."[6]

And that is where a deep knowledge of self lands us in Calvin's view: reaching back to God. If you never really know yourself, he argued, you'll be content with your capacity and abilities. You will never feel your need for God.

Maybe the walls of cynicism, compromise, disconnection, irrelevance, pride, burnout, and emptiness show us the poverty of life apart from God. They do for me. Essentially, these are the things I accomplish unredeemed—untouched by grace and the regenerative work of God. In that way, looking to see what's coming next can be one of the best ways to stay close to a God you're coming to believe in or beginning to love even more deeply. It's a way of acknowledging your weakness, your inability to navigate the complexities of a life you didn't create. It's a plea for direction to a Savior. And I know for me personally, the presence and activity of Jesus in my life is the only thing that has made me more alive and more excited than I've ever been in my life.

And so it comes full circle. Without knowledge of self, there's no knowledge of God. And without knowledge of God, there's no knowledge of self.

With that circle closed, you will be in a far better position to see what's coming.

And, best yet, you'll be ready to deal with it, not alone, but together with a God who created you and who deeply loves you.

Acknowledgments

A book is never a solo venture. Although one name may appear on the cover, there's a tribe of family, friends, and colleagues who have helped to make the message so much better. I learned years ago that life is not so much about what you do; it's about who you do it with. I'm fortunate to get to do it with some of the very finest.

First, to my wife, Toni. You've lived through almost every one of these stories and been so much of the reason I've overcome any of this. God keeps using you again and again to be grace in my life, strength in my walk, and the best friend I could ever imagine having. The times we've had together are the richest I've ever known. God alone knows the long stretches you spent when I was overworking, away speaking, or preoccupied with writing things like this book. But as love does, you keep showing me kindness. You also read every word of this book, over and over, always suggesting the best edits to make this work so much stronger. Thank you. This life is an adventure, and I'm beyond excited about all that's ahead for us.

Then there are my boys, Jordan and Sam, who also lived so much of this material and witnessed my learning process firsthand. Alex, now my beautiful daughter-in-law, has also been a part of this journey since she was in ninth grade. I love the long conversations we have and your new roles not just as my kids but now also as friends and companions on this journey.

The congregation, staff, and elders at Connexus Church continue to amaze me. Thank you for the privilege of building churches that people show up at week after week, year after year. And a particular word of thanks to Jeff Brodie, who stepped into the role I used to hold as lead pastor. He not only rises to the challenges exceedingly well but also continues to let me advise, preach, and be part of this great story as founding pastor. Jeff, I so appreciate your encouragement and support in projects like this and in all that goes on in my life. Thank you.

Reggie Joiner and I have been friends for years, and I've had more meals with him than with anyone in my life I'm not related or married to. The clarity you brought in the Dallas Marriott the night we sat down to dream about this book was exceptional. And thanks for the title. *Didn't See It Coming* was a genius idea. But that should be no surprise to anyone who knows Reggie. I love my Orange/reThink family so much.

Jon Acuff was a great friend in testing ideas, in this and other titles and in so much more. Frank Bealer and Jeff Henderson sat through dinner after dinner, read text after text, and took phone call after phone call during the writing process. Thanks, guys. And thanks to David McDaniel, who is on my personal advisory team and whose imprint on my life at so many critical junctures has been invaluable.

I am so grateful for my team: Sarah Piercy, LeAnne Kelly, Holly Beth Singleton, Dillon Smith, and Lauren Cardwell. You are incredible. Every day you help people thrive in life and leadership. Also many thanks to my web developer, Chris Lema; podcast producer, Toby Lyles; and marketing gurus, Alejandro Reyes and Savannah Sullivan. Although you each have your own company, you know you're part of the team here.

In addition, Jenn Bailey, Marja Nieuwhof (aka Mom), and Sam Nieuwhof all keep the blog and podcast plates spinning so beautifully and keep our little company healthy. Plus, you make it fun in the process. Thank you!

Toni Nieuwhof, Andy Harvey, Jeff Henderson, Frank Bealer, Sarah Piercy, Justin Piercy, Gary Hurst, Jeff Brodie, Jeremy MacDonald, Rich Birch, Dave Douglas, Esther Fedorkevich, and Lauren Hall read the entire manuscript or portions of it, offering helpful feedback and much-appreciated encouragement along the way.

Mark Batterson, my friend, also provided great direction and encouragement early in the writing process. He helps keep my soul and spirit pointing in the right direction. Kevin Jennings is one of the most innovative and encouraging people I know in the marketing world. His ideas have made me so much better. And special thanks also to Lane Jones, who keeps letting me hang out at North Point, even after the lead pastor title disappeared from my business card.

My agent, Esther Fedorkevich, is one of a kind. She, Lauren Hall, and Whitney Gossett have exceeded expectations of what an agency can do for an author. The three of you and the whole team at the Fedd Agency are incredible. How fun that this is only project number one!

And then there's the team at WaterBrook. I have thoroughly enjoyed this entire process. My editor, Andrew Stoddard, quickly became a friend and has been chief enthusiast, encourager, and helper along the way. I am so grateful for all his coaching and wise counsel. Thank you to Kathy Mosier, Keith Wall, and the team for help in editing as well. Many thanks to Alex Field for taking a chance on me. I'm extremely grateful for the partnership and support shown by Tina Constable, Campbell Wharton, and Wade Lucas at Penguin New York. Thanks for taking an interest in a lawyer-turned-pastor-turned-author.

There are about five hundred other people who should also be thanked. Words can't express how grateful I am that my life is rich with so many family members, friends, and colleagues who make it better every day.

Notes

Chapter 1: Find Me a Happy Lawyer

1. See Matthew 16:26.
2. Ecclesiastes 1:18.
3. Thomas Hobbes, *Leviathan* (New York: Penguin Classics, 1985), 186.
4. Jean-Paul Sartre, *No Exit and Three Other Plays* (New York: Vintage, 1989), 45.

Chapter 3: Successful (on the Outside)

1. Stephen R. Covey, *The 7 Habits of Highly Effective People: Powerful Lessons in Personal Change* (New York: Simon and Schuster, 2004), 103–105.
2. Romans 7:15, 18–19, 21–24.

Chapter 4: Taking Your Soul off the Market

1. Blaise Pascal, *Pensées,* trans. A. J. Krailsheimer, rev. ed. (New York: Penguin, 1995), 37.
2. Matthew 7:14.
3. Matthew 7:12.
4. Romans 7:24–25.
5. "10 Research Findings About Deception That Will Blow Your Mind," *Liespotting,* http://liespotting.com/2010/06/10-research-findings -about-deception-that-will-blow-your-mind/; Travis Bradberry, "Sixty Percent of Your Colleagues Are Lying to You," *Huffington Post* (blog),

February 14, 2016, www.huffingtonpost.com/dr-travis-bradberry
/sixty-percent-of-your-col_b_9044758.html.

6. Even a cursory reading of Scripture will show you this is what Jesus
   meant by maturity, but if you're in doubt, read John 13:34–35; 15:12;
   17; and 1 Corinthians 13.

Chapter 5: Is Anyone Out There?

1. Richard Alleyne, "Welcome to the Information Age—174 Newspapers a Day," *Telegraph,* February 11, 2011, www.telegraph.co.uk/news
   /science/science-news/8316534/Welcome-to-the-information-age-174
   -newspapers-a-day.html.

2. Tim Elmore, "What Really Cultivates Self Esteem in Students?"
   Psychology Today, September 19, 2013, www.psychologytoday.com
   /blog/artificial-maturity/201309/what-really-cultivates-self-esteem
   -in-students.

Chapter 6: Ditching Your Phone Won't Help

1. Thomas Edison, quoted in Nathan Furr, "How Failure Taught Edison
   to Repeatedly Innovate," *Forbes,* June 9, 2011, www.forbes.com/sites
   /nathanfurr/2011/06/09/how-failure-taught-edison-to-repeatedly
   -innovate/#11134a5865e9.

2. See Philippians 2:3.

3. Personal conversation with John Ortberg, November 2017. Also see
   John Ortberg, *Soul Keeping: Caring for the Most Important Part of
   You* (Grand Rapids, MI: Zondervan, 2014), 18–21.

Chapter 7: Change Never Asks Permission

1. Rick Warren, "How to Stay Relevant," TEDx talk, October 31, 2012,
   12:41, www.youtube.com/watch?v=LFdRFhVQwvU.

2. Jacqueline Howard, "Here's How Your Taste in Music Evolves as You Age, According to Science," *Huffington Post,* May 21, 2015, www.huffingtonpost.ca/entry/taste-in-music-age_n_7344322.

3. Howard, "Here's How Your Taste in Music Evolves."

Chapter 8: Craving Different

1. I even wrote a book about it, titled *Leading Change Without Losing It* (Cumming, GA: reThink Group, 2012).

2. Scott Anthony, "Kodak's Downfall Wasn't About Technology," *Harvard Business Review,* July 15, 2016, https://hbr.org/2016/07/kodaks-downfall-wasnt-about-technology.

3. Steven Pressfield has written a great book on the resistance people feel to the change they want to make: *Do the Work! Overcome Resistance and Get Out of Your Own Way* (North Egremont, MA: Black Irish Entertainment, 2011).

Chapter 9: It's Not Just the Narcissists

1. Timothy Keller (@timkellernyc), Twitter, September 12, 2014, 2:25 p.m., https://twitter.com/timkellernyc/status/510539614818680832?lang=en.

2. Bobby Ross Jr., "Sex, Money . . . Pride? Why Pastors Are Stepping Down," *Christianity Today,* July 14, 2011, www.christianitytoday.com/ct/2011/julyweb-only/sexmoneypride.html.

3. John Piper, "John Piper's Upcoming Leave," Desiring God, March 28, 2010, www.desiringgod.org/articles/john-pipers-upcoming-leave.

4. John Piper, "I Act the Miracle," Desiring God, February 24, 2011, www.desiringgod.org/messages/i-act-the-miracle.

Chapter 10: Habits of the Humble

1. James 3:13–18.

Chapter 11: Like Falling off a Cliff

1. See Romans 12:15.

Chapter 12: Your New Normal

1. Terry mentored me through a program called Pastors of Excellence, which is no longer active. You can get a sampling of Terry's leadership through his books. See, for example, *Identity Matters: Discovering Who You Are in Christ* (Abilene, TX: Leafwood, 2017).

Chapter 13: When All Your Dreams Come True

1. See 1 Kings 10:21.
2. Ecclesiastes 1:2–8.
3. Ecclesiastes 1:13, 16–18.
4. Carmine Gallo, "70% of Your Employees Hate Their Jobs," *Forbes*, November 11, 2011, www.forbes.com/sites/carminegallo/2011/11/11 /your-emotionally-disconnected-employees.
5. Ecclesiastes 2:1–3.
6. Ecclesiastes 2:4–11.
7. Stephen Adams, "Obesity Killing Three Times as Many as Malnutrition," *Telegraph*, December 13, 2012, www.telegraph.co.uk/news /health/news/9742960/Obesity-killing-three-times-as-many-as -malnutrition.html.
8. Ecclesiastes 1:8.

Chapter 14: My Kingdom Come?

1. Luke 9:24.

Conclusion: Calvin Meets Hobbes

1. John Calvin, *Institutes of the Christian Religion,* ed. John T. McNeill, trans. Ford Lewis Battles (Louisville, KY: Westminster John Knox, 2006), 1:35.

2. See Daniel Goleman, *Emotional Intelligence: Why It Can Matter More Than IQ* (New York: Bantam, 1995).

3. Thanks to my friend Jeff Henderson for that wonderful phrasing. He asks an exceptional self-awareness question of the people around him: "What's it like to be on the other side of me?"

4. See Stephen Mansfield, *10 Signs of a Leadership Crash* (Nashville: Blackwatch Digital, 2017).

5. Calvin, *Institutes,* 1:37.

6. Calvin, *Institutes,* 1:37.

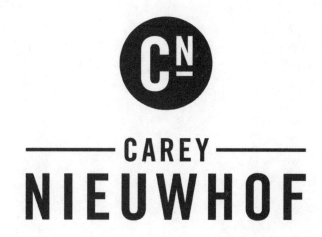